Tragically, teenage suicide is the second leading cause of death among young people today. *Something to Live For*, a sensitive, evocative novel, shows how to step from the shadow of despair into the light of hope. Lissa Halls Johnson includes a "Fact Sheet on Suicide" that alerts you to symptoms of depression and suicide.

By Lissa Halls Johnson
  No Other Choice
  Something to Live For

Lissa Halls Johnson

Something To Live For

Power Books

Fleming H. Revell Company
Old Tappan, New Jersey

Library of Congress Cataloging-in-Publication Data

Johnson, Lissa Halls.
  Something to live for.

  Summary: When Kerry's family moves to a distant state and her dream of
becoming a professional singer with her best friend Justine seems to be faltering,
the separation and disappointment tests their faith in God and leads one of them
to suicide.
  [1. Suicide—Fiction. 2. Friendship—Fiction. 3. Singers—Fiction.
4. Christian life—Fiction.]
  I. Title.
PZ7.J63253So 1986   [Fic]   86-17818
ISBN 0-8007-5228-7 (pbk.)

Copyright © 1986 by Lissa Halls Johnson
Published by the Fleming H. Revell Company
Old Tappan, New Jersey 07675
Printed in the United States of America

For my children,
Trevor, Stacie, and Misty.
May you always find something to live for,
a reason to celebrate life.
I love you.

Something To Live For

❧ 1 ❧

❧Justine sat rigid in the metal folding chair, sucking in deep breaths, and counting to three before letting them out again. Her feet rested flat on the floor, coming to life every few seconds, tapping furtive rhythms on the dusty floor. She looked over at Kerry, her smile a feeble attempt at excitement.

Kerry perched on the edge of her chair, ready to fly on stage the moment their turn arrived. Her heels, hooked on the chair rung beneath her, squeaked whenever she moved.

"I'm so nervous," Justine whispered.

Kerry grinned, her blue eyes catching the light. "I'm excited," she whispered back.

Justine shook her head. *She's crazy*, she thought. *We're*

*going to perform in front of six hundred of our classmates, and she's
not even nervous!*

Jack Florez leaned into the podium, his hands moving
with his words. Tall and too skinny to be terribly good
looking, his easy manner and sense of humor pushed him
into the slot of most popular guy at Central High. His jokes
slid out of his mouth like the comedian Justine had seen on
TV the night before. She wondered where the talent came
from. His cousin Marsha was the boringest kid around.

"Following the skit performed by Mr. Craig's drama
class," Jack announced, "Justine Crawford and Kerry Reynolds will sing an original song written by Kerry."

As Jack left the stage, he gave Kerry a thumbs-up sign.
She smiled coolly at him, as though she had performed a
thousand times. *Kerry was born to do this stuff,* Justine thought.
I'll take the fortune, and she can have the fame.

The skit droned on, nobody laughing when they were
supposed to. "Whoever cast Marsha as the leading lady
sure goofed," Kerry whispered. "Her voice is so, so . . ."

". . . monotone," Justine whispered back.

Kerry nodded vigorously.

Marsha forgot her lines three times, as did her leading
man. The butler totally breached stage etiquette, and said
his lines with his back turned toward the audience.

The crowd clapped—short, slow claps of obligation.
"Well, we're next," Kerry said, excitement shaking her
voice.

Justine nodded, staring at the stage as the curtains closed
and the stage crew removed the few stage props. They set
two stools and a microphone in the middle of the stage.
Mike, the stage director, waved them over. The crowd was
getting noisy. A few guys made loud catcalls. Justine's
hands shook. "I'll never get used to this."

"Oh, sure you will," Kerry replied. "This is fun!"

"You call getting sick fun?"

"Shhh . . ."

The heavy damask curtains swooshed back. Justine forced herself to smile. The restless audience moved about, whispering to one another. Some of the guys whistled and shouted, "Come on, baby! Sing it out now, sing it!"

Justine wanted to bolt, but Kerry had already begun strumming the guitar.

> *It may not sound to you, like the sparrow can sing,*
> *but his heart is bursting with song.*

Kerry's top-shape voice carried the song. Justine sang the harmony, their voices blending well. The crowd hushed.

When they finished the song, applause rippled through the auditorium. As the curtains closed, the girls could hear someone in the audience shouting, "More! More!" The request hatched more shouts, until the whole auditorium seemed caught up in the demand. Kerry looked at Justine. "See! I told you they'd love us!"

Jack's voice boomed over the microphone. "Because of the time limit, we cannot have an encore."

The crowd began to shout in unison, "More! More!" clapping and stomping feet in rhythm.

Jack stuck his head around the curtain. "Well, girls. Can you do another song?"

Kerry nodded. "Of course!"

Jack smiled. "This time don't do such a good job. We've got to let that guy who thinks he's funny have a turn. Come to think of it, be extra good, then maybe we can tell him there's not enough time for him."

Kerry tipped her head back and laughed.

Justine rolled her eyes. "Thanks a lot, Kerry. I finally got over being scared as the curtains were closing, and now you've gone and done it again."

"You won't have to be so scared this time. Let's do 'Edelweiss' for old times' sake."

11

The curtains rolled back, and Justine saw a multitude of friendly faces. Instead of being distracted, and talking to each other, the audience was in full attention. Every face looked up at them, waiting to have their senses pleased again.

As Justine sang, she felt the anxiety slip away. There seemed to be nothing more wonderful in this world. Nothing more wonderful than music, than a song well sung. To warm your heart and to lift your spirit.

She felt her voice swell with Kerry's, the two in perfect rhythm. She felt the tears trickle down her face as they always did when she sang this song.

With the final strum of the guitar, both girls dropped their heads, and the curtains closed. The silence hung in the air, and Justine felt her heart beat faster. "They hated us," she whispered to Kerry.

Kerry shook her head, beaming. Just then, the applause came, like thunder. "You always know when you've done your best. The crowd is stunned. The applause comes later. Come on, let's go take a bow."

Kerry grabbed Justine's hand and pulled her through the curtains. The guitar's bridge caught on the curtain, dragging it along with them. Kerry ignored it, bowing happily to their friends in the audience. Then she unhooked the guitar, and they disappeared backstage.

Jack introduced the comedian, then slipped back, grabbing Kerry's arm. "Hey, you were terrific!"

"Thanks, Jack."

Justine watched Kerry's blue eyes take on the puppy-dog look of adoration. It was a killer. No guy could resist that look. Kerry didn't seem to notice she even did it. She didn't realize she wrinkled up her freckled nose when she thought deeply, either. All of her bubbly movements were natural. Nothing put on. Always happy, always letting the yucky things of life roll off her back.

Not like me, Justine thought wistfully. *I can't let anything roll off my back. Express it now, forget it later. That's my motto.*

Jack sat in a metal folding chair, his arms crossed, staring at the "funny man" who got a few dry laughs. He looked at Kerry, who sat on the edge of her chair. She seemed to be mentally encouraging the guy to do a good job. She loved for performers to do well, but after they'd had a few chances, and then failed, she wasn't quite so kind—like with Marsha.

Jack stared at Kerry; Justine stared at Jack. "Kerry," he finally whispered.

Kerry turned her head, a wry smile playing on her lips. "Yeah?"

"Will you go out with me Friday night?"

Kerry looked at him a moment. "Where?"

Jack thought. "Ice-skating?"

"Okay." She turned back to the comedian as if nothing had happened.

After the show, everyone shuffled out of the auditorium, heading reluctantly back to class. "Kerry," Justine said, "you acted like you didn't care one bit if you went out with Jack or not."

"Of course I care," Kerry retorted. "I was so surprised, and so nervous, I didn't know what to say."

"*You* were nervous?"

"I know, can you believe it? I guess it's because I've wanted to go out with Jack for so long. I never thought he'd even look at me. My pudgy legs would scare anybody off."

"Oh, would you quit it with your pudgy legs bit? You aren't fat."

"But I am at least thirty pounds overweight."

"Try fifteen. I've seen you on the scale. If you lost thirty pounds you'd be that sparrow you were singing about."

"Okay, I'll settle for twenty . . . for right now. Do you think I could lose at least five pounds by Friday?"

Justine rolled her eyes. "No, Kerry, I don't think so. I don't think you should kill yourself trying, either."

"But Jack is so skinny. Don't you think he'd be embarrassed to be seen skating with a fat girl?" Kerry pinched her legs, her nose wrinkled in disgust.

"He asked you out fifteen pounds over. I doubt he expects you to lose it all before Friday. Now, would you stop worrying about it? We're going to be late to class."

"Yeah, I guess so. I've been late twice already to biology. Mr. Wright said he'd give me a detention if I was late once more. See you after school, okay?"

***

The next morning, as she walked up the street to Kerry's pink stucco house, Justine puffed little breath clouds out in front of her. She knocked on the door, her knuckles hurting with each knock. Kerry peeked out the door, then threw it open wide. "Come on in. I'll be just a couple more minutes."

Justine felt as if she had been put into an oven. "What do you guys keep your thermostat set on, anyway?" Justine asked, as Kerry put finishing touches of mascara on her long lashes. "Oh, my parents keep it at a frosty sixty-eight degrees, so as soon as they leave in the morning, I turn it up to seventy-six, or something like that."

"I'm roasting."

"Ummm, not me. This is just right. Okay, I'm ready. Let me turn the heat back down, and we can go."

Kerry locked the door behind her. "Brrr, it's freezing out here."

"Good grief, Kerry. It's forty degrees outside. I'd hate to see you back East. They'd laugh you right out of there. Forty is shirt-sleeve weather for most Easterners."

"Good for them. It's freezing to me. The cold weather does terrible things to my voice. When I see puffs of my

14

own breath, it's too cold." Kerry pulled her jacket up around her throat. "Besides, I thought Los Angeles was never supposed to be cold."

"You've lived here long enough to know better than that."

Kerry pouted. "I still think the chamber of commerce is telling lies to people."

"Oh, Kerry, you're crazy." Justine laughed.

"Speaking of crazy, I've started a new diet. I only eat grapefruit for breakfast and dinner. For lunch I eat carrots and celery, maybe some cheese for protein. Pretty good, huh?" Kerry slid her free hand down her side. "I should lose at least three pounds the first week."

"Where'd you get that crazy diet?"

"I read about it in the paper. I changed it a little bit though. I added more grapefruit since it's supposed to be the best thing to lose weight."

"How about exercise?"

"Exercise? What's that? Oh, Justine, you know I always fail P.E. I'm a klutz. I hate sports. That's why I'm glad Jack asked me out and not George, or Pete from the football team. I couldn't stand being with a jock all night."

"But you'll ice-skate? That's exercise, a sport."

"No it's not." Kerry bounced up ahead and spun around. "It's fun."

Justine shook her head. "Kerry, sometimes you mix me all up."

Kerry laughed. "Funny, that's what my mom says."

Justine walked for a while, then shivered.

"Have you thought anymore about what you want to do next year?" Kerry asked her.

"No. Maybe I'll work with handicapped kids someday. An occupational therapist or something." She tilted her head to one side, thinking. "Maybe I'd rather sing, but Grandma says there's no future in that."

Kerry threw back her head and shouted, "Hah! Let me tell you, there's a future where we're going."

A smirk passed across Justine's face. "We?"

"Of course *we.*" Kerry's triumphant face fell a little. "That is, after college, if my mom has her way." Kerry plucked the corner of her Peechee folder. "Have you sent off any college applications?"

"Not yet. I don't know if I even want to go straight to college. I'm tired of school." Justine smiled and looked around as if ready to tell a secret. "There's too much life to live and school stifles it."

Kerry nodded her understanding. "My mom is driving me nuts. She thinks I should apply to UCLA or some crazy thing. She'd even like me to go to Occidental College. But if you think I'm going to go to the college right across the street from my house, you're as crazy as she is." She reached up and grabbed a leaf off a tree, admiring the flaming fall colors in it.

Justine pulled her drooping purse strap back on her shoulder. "My folks would push me harder to go to college, but they don't have the money. So if I really want to go, it will be out of my pocket. I don't know. I guess I just don't care right now. I don't want to crowd out the fun of my senior year by getting too serious. Serious destroys the outlook. Know what I mean?"

"Oh, I don't think so. I'd better be awfully serious if my career in singing and songwriting is going to go anywhere."

"You've been serious all your life about singing. I guess it hasn't hurt you any. Hey, are we still going to sing for that group your mom belongs to?"

Kerry drew her brows together. "You mean for her old friends from Delta Chi?"

Justine nodded. "I guess that's them. I can never remember the name."

"Mom said they're still trying to decide. Since they've

16

never heard us, they aren't sure we're any good. You know Mom. She brags on me so much that people think she's just a proud, pushy mother."

"She *is* a proud, pushy mother."

"True, true."

"You know, Kerry, sometimes I think I'd like to hear my voice on the radio, or hear my songs being sung, but I don't know. Don't you have to be somebody first?"

"I think you have to know somebody. Claudia always says you have to have a gimmick, or a great voice. Well, I certainly don't have a gimmick unless you want to call me Fat Sue and Her Singing Sparrows or something like that. So I've been trying for the great voice."

Justine looked for cars, then stepped into the street. "You've already got the great voice."

"I'm working on it. I've got so much more work to do before I can truly say I have a great voice. But my voice sounds much better when you sing with me. You know that, don't you?"

"You've told me that enough times, I'd better know it. We do sound okay sometimes, don't we?"

Kerry hopped up on the opposite curb. "Yes, we do. We're going to make it, aren't we?"

Justine laughed. "Now you sound like the old Mary Tyler Moore shows. But yeah, I think we can make it. We'll make your dream come true. I like dreams."

"So why don't you have any?"

"It's too much bother, and yours are more interesting."

The bell rang as they walked up the front steps of the school. A chiseled concrete sign said CENTRAL HIGH. The "Avenues" and the "Delevan Boys" had sprayed their graffiti all over it, announcing who loved who, and which gang was better than which.

"Stupid fools," Justine muttered.

"See you in English," Kerry said.

❧ 2 ❧

❧ **K**erry drove her mother's gold Impala through the streets of the Valley, amazed that her parents had finally let her come by herself. "I guess Mom finally decided a day at the beach with her friend Sally took precedence over her fear I'll get creamed on the freeway."

Kerry turned the radio up full blast, and began to warm up her voice. She sang quiet and low at first, stretching her vocal cords as a runner stretches her legs. Only once had she made the mistake of not warming up before voice lessons. Claudia knew immediately, and spent fifteen minutes of Kerry's precious singing time lecturing on the importance of warming up, and the disasters that can happen to singers who don't take care of their instruments.

Kerry never forgot to warm up now. She even warmed up before each performance, each practice. She wanted to keep her voice a good working instrument forever.

She drove up the driveway, past the white clapboard house to the detached garage in back. Taking the sheet music and the blank cassette from the worn seat, she stepped out of the car. Her blond hair had been pulled back into a scarlet ribbon, the front pieces hanging down like a shaggy dog's. Putting the music and tape on the hood of the car, she bent down to tie her gray Nikes.

She took a deep breath before heading through the gate, and fought off three dogs and two cats who greeted her like an old friend. She knocked twice, then opened the door.

Claudia stopped playing the piano as Kerry walked in. "Kerry! How nice to see you." Kerry felt Claudia's soft arms around her, the faint smell of gardenias drifting past along with Claudia's auburn hair.

"Anything exciting happening at school these days? How did you do in the talent show?" Claudia asked as she returned to the piano.

Kerry smiled. "Justine and I did so well, they asked for an encore!"

Claudia swept over, and gave Kerry another hug. "I'm so proud of you. Now when do I get to meet this mysterious Justine? I've heard about her every week for a year, and I've yet to meet her."

"Maybe in a few weeks? She usually makes plans for Wednesdays knowing I'm going to be coming out here."

"A few weeks it is. I want your promise on that!"

"I promise, Claudia."

"One more thing, before we get started. Have you applied to Indiana University's School of Music?"

"You mean Bloomington's?"

Claudia nodded.

Kerry hung her head. "Not yet. I'm not sure I want to go to college yet."

Claudia clucked like a mother hen. "If you want to go as far as you wish with your music, you should reach for the best. And the best for you, would be Bloomington's."

"I don't know, Claudia. My schoolwork comes hard enough as it is. I don't know if I could tackle college."

"Sure you could. We'd better get to work now."

Kerry popped her cassette tape into the machine, punching the record button. As Claudia played, Kerry sang the scales several times, up and down.

"You've warmed up well, Kerry. Today, I decided we'll work on your high notes. Since your voice tends to be in the alto range, you need to work on slipping into the higher notes with less effort."

Claudia began to sing a series of high notes, using pure vowel sounds. "Now join me."

Kerry followed along.

"Don't try so hard, Kerry. Ease into it. That's right."

The half hour passed quickly, but when it was over, Kerry felt she had just finished playing tennis. She was worn out. She turned off the tape recorder and removed the tape.

Claudia turned to her, resting one arm on the top of the piano. "How often do you practice, Kerry?"

"At least once a day. Sometimes twice on the weekends."

Claudia smiled. "It shows, Kerry. I think you'll make it if you continue to work this hard."

A celebration went off in Kerry's mind, but she couldn't let Claudia know. "I hope I'll see my dream, Claudia. But I'm only an ordinary kid. You have to be somebody special to make it in the music world."

Claudia took a stack of brightly colored bracelets from the piano and slipped them onto her pale arm. Her warm face pulled together in thought. "Sometimes people who make it are special only because they have the right connections, or enough money. But the ones who make it because they can sing—really sing—are ordinary people, like you, who had a dream they never let go of. Hold on to your dream, Kerry. Don't let it go."

Kerry slid into the car, buckled in, and popped an old Amy Grant tape into the tape deck. Her thoughts circled Claudia's last words, examining them and rejoicing over them. As she backed out of the driveway, Amy's voice filled the car. Kerry joined her, her heart soaring with the birds that scattered above her. She didn't care that the kids in the car next to her at the stoplight laughed and pointed as she sang.

Whenever Kerry sang, whenever she was carried away by the song, she felt closer to something. To Justine, to God, to nature. Something inside seemed to break loose and give her life meaning. Most of the time, life seemed to swirl around in eddies of confusion. What to do after graduation in June. What to do after life begins in six months. What to wear, how to handle the scary things happening in the world. She hated those feelings of confusion and loneliness. The world could get too ugly to face. But with her songs, the problems all faded away, and she could feel the true beauty that the Creator had intended.

As she pulled onto the bogged freeway, she turned off the tape and improvised, using her instrument to the best of its ability.

> O Lord, my precious Lord,
> I'm here to sing Your praise.
> You have given me a song to sing,
> To rejoice in each of Your days.
> I will sing to Your glory.
> I will sing to Your people.
> I will sing to all the world,
> The creation of Your love.

She says You've given me a gift, dear Lord, a gift to sing Your songs. Help me to follow my dream, dear God, the dream You've given me.

She smiled at the scowling faces next to her, as people jostled and fought for a place in the traffic. The cars inched forward, almost like little kids pushing and shoving in a movie theater line.

Kerry turned the tape back on, enjoying every minute of the traffic. In it she could have more time to sing, with her music on as loud as she pleased—no mother, no father, whining for her to turn it down.

Her heart skipped a beat every so often as a car leapt in front of her without warning. But her song kept on, her dreams burning with a newly fueled flame.

The next day was a gorgeous, warm fall day. So many of the fall days in Los Angeles were enough to make anyone fall in love with the sprawling city. The few trees that could, had turned colors, their crisp leaves skittering along in the wind. They liked to play chase and follow, but hated to get caught under an inconsiderate foot.

The sky had turned so blue, and the puffy clouds wandered overhead.

Justine's brown eyes shone when Kerry told her of Claudia's invitation. "She really wants to meet me?"

"Yeah. She even said we could change the practice for one day. Instead of doing my exercises, we could sing a few songs for her, and she'd help us work on them."

Justine pulled back a little. "I don't know, Kerry. I don't know if I could sing in front of a famous voice teacher. What if she laughs at my voice?"

"She's not going to laugh, Justine. You have a terrific voice, and you know it."

Justine shifted her load of books to her left arm. "My voice is a lot better than some people's, but good enough for a famous voice teacher to tolerate it?"

"Stop it with the famous-voice-teacher junk." Kerry crinkled her nose over a crooked smile. "She's a nice lady. Nice ladies know how to be civil when the situation demands. When she hears how lousy you are, she'll be civil."

Justine laughed. "Kerry, you always have a way with words."

"It's my job, you know." Kerry smiled.

As the girls approached the school, a car pulled up next to them. "Want a ride to school?" a friendly voice called.

Justine was about to say no when she saw it was Jack. She looked at Kerry, who grinned shyly. "I guess so, but we're only two blocks away."

"You need to save your energy," he said.

Justine opened the door of the brown Toyota, climbing into the backseat. "I'm lazy," she said. "I'll ride."

Kerry climbed into the front seat, her face red. "Thanks, Jack. This is nice of you."

"Anytime. As a matter of fact, I was wondering if I could come pick you up in the morning from your house?" He shifted gears, looking sideways at her, keeping one eye on the road.

"I don't know," she paused. She turned to look at Justine. Justine tried not to look apprehensive. She didn't feel like walking to school alone every day, yet she certainly wasn't going to butt in on this opportunity for Kerry to get to know Jack.

Jack honked, then swerved to avoid hitting a group of kids who stepped out in front of him. "I don't know why they think they are indestructible," he said angrily. "They don't obey a red light, thinking they have all the rights in the world, and no one else deserves any respect."

As he pulled into the parking lot, and into a space, he said to Kerry, "So, what do you think?"

Justine opened the door, slipping out to let Kerry decide on her own.

Jack's voice called to her. "Wait a minute, Justine. Don't you live close to Kerry?"

Justine nodded.

"You could have a ride, too, if you want. I'll just pick you up at Kerry's house."

"Thanks, Jack, but I don't want to be an intruding pest or anything."

Jack wrinkled his forehead. "Why would you be a pest? Do you smell or something?"

Justine laughed. "Never mind. I'd love to. It's up to Kerry."

Relieved that Jack had asked Justine to join them, Kerry said, "Tell you what, Jack. I'll let you know on Monday."

"Oh, ho! You want to see how the date goes first—to see if I'm as creepy as I look."

Kerry snapped to her old self. "You are so right, Jack. I didn't want to say yes, and find out how weird you really are, and be stuck riding with you."

Jumping out of the car, Jack ran around to open Kerry's door. "Mademoiselle," he said with a sweeping bow, "you will only be riding with the best chauffeur in town. But you do as you wish, and give me your answer on Monday."

Justine waved and walked away. As she did, Jack got a bit more serious. "Kerry, I'll be at your house tomorrow night at seven. I want to meet your dad before we go. The skating session doesn't start until eight."

"You want to meet my dad? Are you serious? My dad is the worst person when it comes to my dates."

"Why is that?"

"Maybe because I'm an only child. They treat me like I'm a piece of Mother's antique china. You know the story. 'No one is good enough for my little girl.' "

Waving his hand, Jack assured her, "Don't worry about me, I'll just turn on the charm."

"Do you have any?" Kerry teased.

"Not really. I'll have to study up on it tonight."

Jack touched Kerry's elbow lightly as she went up the steps. A wonderful warmth shot through her arm. *He dropped his hand too soon,* she thought. She turned and looked at him with an encouraging smile, hoping there would be more the next night.

***

The following evening, the wind toyed with Kerry's hair as Jack opened the door for her. She felt a little silly, and a little nice that he would be so old-fashioned. As Jack started the car he looked at her, smiling. "You look real nice, Kerry," he said.

Kerry blushed, glad he couldn't tell in the dark. So many guys lied to her about her looks, she knew. But Jack was too sincere, his voice too stern to be joking. "Thanks. You look nice too."

The drive to the skating rink could have been as uncomfortable as all Kerry's other dates. She hated herself for turning into a different person the moment she was alone with a guy. She got all shy and never knew what to say. The minute he dropped her off at home, she thought of a thousand witty things to say, and interesting questions to ask.

Unlike the others, Jack took the silence like an unmolded piece of clay, and began to work it gently, letting it sit, and then working on it again.

"Have you ice-skated before?" he asked.

"Yes. One summer my dad took us every weekend."

"Uh-oh, then that means you're really good."

Kerry smiled. "It only means I can skate fast. I never took any lessons, so the only thing I learned how to do was skate faster."

"Can you skate backwards?"

"Nope."

Jack let out an obvious, phony sigh. Then he talked

softly, as if to himself. "Good, I'd hate to have her show me up on the first date."

Kerry laughed an easy laugh. She felt her normal self returning, with only a little awkwardness left.

The parking lot was only half full when they arrived. "Great!" Jack exclaimed, thumping the steering wheel. "It shouldn't be crowded tonight. I hate fighting all those stumbling little kids . . ."

Kerry nodded knowingly.

". . . they always make me fall."

The unexpected comment brought out a huge, unladylike guffaw from Kerry. Jack turned, his smile saying how pleased he was that he had touched her funny bone as he intended.

Inside the rink, Kerry didn't see much of what went on around her. She was so nervous, she could hardly tie her rental skates. Jack tied his with firm speed. He looked at her struggles, and scooted close to her. Without a word, he bent down and took the frayed strings from her hands. He lifted her leg across his, and with the same firm speed, he tied both her skates too.

Kerry looked at him, amazed. First he handled her dad like she'd never seen anyone do before. Now he helped her, without making a silly comment that would have embarrassed her. Guys could make you feel so dumb. Why did Jack know what to do?

Jack held her hand, sending wonderful, welcome feelings straight to her heart. It was nice to belong to someone, even if only for the moment.

The night passed too quickly for both of them. At Kerry's door, they laughed over their sore, wobbly ankles.

As their laughter died in self-consciousness, Kerry looked up at Jack, afraid at what she would see there. She had gotten used to the hungry, demanding look in her dates' eyes. A false Bambi look.

Green eyes that seemed to be smiling met hers.

"I've had such a wonderful time, Kerry. I hope you'll go out with me again."

Kerry's stiff fear left her. "I've never had a nicer time, Jack. I'd love to go out with you again."

Jack kissed her gently on the cheek, opened the door for her, and left.

***

"You didn't call me last night, you turkey," Justine complained. She hung onto the phone with her shoulder as she filed her nails. "So how'd it go with Jack? Is he as nice as he seems? Did he kiss you? Did he hold your hand?"

"Calm down, Justine. I didn't call you last night because I got home too late. I thought you'd realize that."

"I waited up till eleven. . . ."

"I didn't get home until eleven-thirty." Kerry pushed her hair out of her eyes and held it on top of her head.

"So? How was it?" Justine asked impatiently.

Kerry pulled her nightgown over her knees, leaning against the wall. "Ummm, it was wonderful. Jack is terrific!"

"I know that already, so tell me about last night."

"When he picked me up, of course Dad had to check him out to make sure he was okay. I thought I'd die. But Jack was so cool, he knew just what to say. He even asked Dad about his job and stuff!"

"You're kidding?"

"I'm tellin' ya, he even had my dad laughing!"

"So did you ever leave?"

"Of course, silly. But you know, it's the first time my dad has ever given the seal of approval."

"What's that?"

"He said, 'What time do you think you'll be home?' Not, 'You will be home by. . . .' He actually let Jack decide!"

"So what'd Jack say?" Justine asked.

"He looked Dad straight in the eye—I can't even do that—and said, 'What time do you want her home, sir?'"

"Sir?"

"Yeah, Justine, I thought I'd pop. Dad told him twelve-thirty!"

"So why did you come home early?"

"That was Jack's idea too. He said if he kept bringing me home an hour early, that one day when we wanted to stay out later than curfew, Dad would probably be more willing."

"Give that man a medal."

"Skating wasn't half bad either. We skated almost the whole time, except twice he bought me hot chocolate to keep me warm and my energy up."

"Are you sure Jack is for real?"

"I don't know, but I'll take him anyway."

❧ 3 ❧

❧Justine tucked her favorite blouse into her jeans. The tiny white seagulls flew over the pale blue fabric. She brushed her hair again, pulling it back on one side, fastening it high on her head with a white shell alligator clip. She put on another coat of mascara, and retouched the blush on her high cheekbones. She pushed at her nose, wishing it would sink into her face just a little bit. It was too long, and too wide. Someday, she planned to take a course in makeup. Then maybe she could learn all the tricks of making it look smaller.

The old wood floor creaked as she ran back to her bedroom to put her shoes on. The doorbell rang, and her nerves shivered.

"I'll be there in a minute, Kerry," she called. She grabbed her hoop earrings and stuck them in her ears. As she ran out of the room, she grabbed her purse.

"Hurry," Kerry's muffled voice called. "We can't be late."

As Justine rushed out the front door, locking it behind her, she asked, "Do I look okay, Kerry?"

"You look awfully dressed up."

"I didn't know what to wear to meet a famous voice teacher." Justine noticed Kerry wore a lavender jogging suit.

"Claudia doesn't care what you wear, she only cares how you sing."

"I guess I hoped that if I sang rotten, she'd at least be nice to me because I'm not dressed like a slob."

Shaking her head, Kerry said, "Stop worrying, you'll do fine, just so long as you warm up."

Kerry put her last week's lesson in the tape deck. Both girls sang along with it, starting out slow and easy, building to a steady sound. "See?" Kerry said. "You sound terrific."

"That's your opinion."

It surprised Justine to see that a famous voice teacher lived in such a modest house.

"I think she spends all her money on the studio," Kerry told her. "It's acoustically correct and everything. Wait till you see it."

Kerry stopped outside the garage. "Where is the studio?" Justine asked.

"You're looking at it."

"A garage? I thought you said it was nice."

"It is. Be patient."

Justine talked to the dogs and the cats, one by one, trying to avoid the person on the other side of the door. She asked each their names until Kerry caught on. Kerry simply knocked on the door and walked in. Justine stood up and followed her.

"Kerry! How nice to see you!" Claudia called in her musical voice. "And you're Justine." She gave each girl a hug.

Feeling awkward and smothered, Justine looked at Kerry, and noticed the hug had changed her face a bit. Now she looked more at ease, a little bit at home.

Claudia moved and breathed in a flowing, controlled way. She wore a loose-fitting skirt and blouse, flowers and butterflies all over them. The skirt flowed with her every movement, trailing after her as she moved from one part of the room to the other. Each hand motion was strong and sure, yet airy and light.

Justine wondered if Claudia was all put on, or if music had become a part of her, taking over her movements and voice. Everything she did seemed musical.

Looking around the room, Justine noticed that from the inside you couldn't tell you were in a garage. A dusty-rose-colored carpet covered the floor. It matched the tiny roses flecked on the cream wallpaper. Here and there hung photographs of Claudia's students—the famous and the unknown. A picture of Kerry hung near the piano. Hers was the only color photograph. All the others had been professionally photographed in black and white, the famous ones bearing a brief note and autograph. "Without you, Claudia . . .," most of them began, ". . . I never would have made it."

A couch, matching the carpet, sat in one end of the room. It had a small smoked-glass coffee table in front of it.

A clock hung above it, its gold pendulum moving back and forth, silently ticking away the minutes of each pupil's lesson.

The baby grand piano stood majestically in the center of the room. Two stools stood next to it, one with a tape recorder perched on top of it.

Justine didn't pay much attention to Kerry's chatter to Claudia about her new song. Her ears perked up when Claudia asked them to sing a song they had written together.

After scales, Kerry put the handwritten sheet music in front of Claudia. Claudia played it through a few times, and seemed then to have played it many times before.

Her heart thumping wildly in her chest, Justine didn't think she had felt this nervous about any performance she had ever done. She sang quietly at first, then, as she sang the words she believed in, her voice became clearer and stronger. Looking at each other, she and Kerry watched for the changes in tempo, melody, and harmony. With the song completed, Justine hung her head, afraid to look at Claudia.

"Well, girls," she said softly. "You have done a fine job. Now let's sing it from the chorus. I think you need to change some of your harmony. It isn't working as well as it could."

For the next twenty minutes, Justine worked more than she had ever dreamed possible. Many times they sang one section over and over, concentrating, sometimes, on the sound of just one letter or group of notes. It made her feel she'd never get it right, and it was useless to try.

"Okay, girls, let's sing it through once more before you go."

As Justine sang, her mind concentrated on each word, each note, each sound of each letter. She could tell Kerry, too, was intense in her concentration.

Claudia played the final notes with a flourish. She turned off the tape recorder. "See how much better it sounded that time?"

Justine didn't see at all, but she nodded anyway. Her head ached a bit, and she wished she still carried the tin of aspirin with her. She would have swallowed all the little crumbled pieces right then.

"See you next week, Kerry," Claudia said, as though she had done no work at all. "And Justine, I'm so glad to have met you. Kerry tells me how much you encourage her, and I can see why. You too have a talent that shouldn't be ignored. If you want it to blossom and grow, give your mom my card, and I'll be happy to give you lessons too." She pressed the card into Justine's hand and shooed them out the door.

Once in the car, Kerry rewound the tape. "Here's our song the first time we sang it."

Justine listened and smiled. "Not bad, huh?"

Kerry fast-forwarded it, finding the spot she wanted. "And here's the last time we sang it."

Justine's jaw dropped open as she listened. "Wow, Claudia's right! That sounds so much better."

"Amazing, isn't it?"

"Do you think I should take lessons from Claudia?" Justine asked.

Kerry's face lit up. "Do you really think you could? I think that would be wonderful. We could go out together like today, and have our lessons back to back."

"And maybe Claudia would let us work on one of our songs each time at the end of the lesson."

"We'll get so good, that all the record labels will be begging for us to sing for them."

"And then we'll be rich!" Justine exclaimed.

"And then we'll be famous," whispered Kerry.

"Now all we have to do is convince my mom."

"You'll have to let her know how serious you are," Kerry added.

"I've never been serious about anything in my life. I can't even be serious about my future."

Kerry looked over her shoulder and pulled onto the freeway. "But you have to work on the future now. You'll never reach your goals if you don't work now."

"My, don't you sound grown-up."

Kerry blushed. "It's all that time I've spent with Claudia. She reminds me over and over how it's hard work that reaches goals."

"So why aren't you going to go to college?"

"I'm not good enough, Justine. I'm just a slob who works her brains out and still only gets Bs. I can't even get an A in music, my best subject."

"Have you ever talked to Mr. Belton about that?"

"Yeah, didn't I tell you? He said that if I were an ordinary kid, I'd get As for the work I'm doing. But because I have such a 'gift,' such a 'talent,' he thought I should be doing better."

"You're kidding! What a jerk. I'm so glad he thinks I'm an ordinary kid."

"No kidding," Kerry said, spitting out her words. "You get As when you don't even try. I don't think that's fair."

Looking out the window, Justine waved at a ponytailed redhead in the car next to them, whose nose pressed against the window, making her look like a little pig. Justine hated these conversations. She couldn't help how easy school-work came to her, any more than Kerry could help getting Bs when she worked harder than anyone.

"Are you and Jack going out Friday night?" Justine asked after a few silent minutes. She hoped changing the subject might help get Kerry out of her troubled thoughts.

A slow smile took over Kerry's face. "You bet. We're going ice-skating again."

"Is that all you guys ever do?"

"Seems like it sometimes. We're going Saturday night too."

"I wish I had a date," Justine complained. "I guess I'm just so beautiful that I intimidate all the men."

Laughing, Kerry said, "Hey, that reminds me. We're going to see that new Dudley Moore movie on a Saturday night in a couple of weeks. Want to come?"

"I'd better not . . ." Justine answered. But she did want to go. She loved to laugh, and Dudley Moore always made her laugh.

"Please come. Jack has been saying he wants you to go with us somewhere sometime."

"Because he feels sorry for me? That no one will ask me out?"

Kerry snorted. "Jack doesn't feel sorry for you. He just thinks it's silly for us to always go out alone, when our friends could come along and share the fun."

"Are any of his friends coming along?"

Kerry turned the radio up. "I *love* this song. I think he asked Pete and Larry. I'm not sure. Come anyway, okay? Jack wants to get to know you better, and I want you to get to know him."

"You really like him, don't you, Kerry?"

Twisting her hair around her fingers, Kerry smiled. "I do. He's so . . . human. He understands my ponderings."

"He does? I can't even follow them. I can't see any use in pondering. It only takes up time. Let things happen as they happen. Let them be what they are."

"But thinking hard helps me to understand things. I can control my emotions better. I don't have to get angry, because I can see why people do things when I think about it from their point of view."

Justine shrugged her shoulders. "I don't see what's wrong in getting mad. Scream, yell, throw a book against a wall. It makes me feel better."

Kerry shook. "Oh, I couldn't do that. It might destroy the book. Besides, there's nothing worth really getting mad over."

"What about getting sad? Don't you ever cry? I can't remember the last time I saw you cry."

Kerry laughed. "I cry sometimes, but I don't usually let anyone know. If I cry, it only shows I'm feeling sorry for myself. I just tell myself it isn't really that bad, that other people have it worse than I do."

"You really think that?"

"Well, I realize I shouldn't cry when one of my demo tapes is refused. Other people have been rejected before, and they lived through it, so, so should I."

Justine shook her head. "I can't go along with that. Hey, when life isn't fair, I cry, I yell at God, I tell Him what I think of Him."

"But Justine, don't you think God only brings stuff into your life that is good for you?"

"Let's say I disagree with His judgment a lot."

Kerry pulled up in front of Justine's house. "Let me know about going to the movie. And say hello to Joey for me, okay? Tell him to give Mister Rogers a kiss for me."

"Oh, Kerry. You can be so gross! See you tomorrow."

Justine bounced happily into the house.

"Justine?" her mom called from the kitchen. "Come tell me about it."

"Oh, Mom, it was wonderful. It was such hard work, but we got so much better. I'll have to let you listen to the tape Kerry made of us singing. Claudia said she thought I was good and that she'd like to teach me."

"Great! Here, cut these." She put a bag of green beans on the cutting board, pulling Justine over to them. "Do you want to take voice lessons?"

"Oh, yes! Kerry and I could have back-to-back lessons, and then we could sing one of our songs at the end, and get so much better that we could really see our dream come true of becoming recording artists."

Justine's mother laughed. "We'll have to talk to your father, and talk to the teacher. It depends on how much it costs. I've been thinking about getting a part-time job in Kelly's Gift Shop anyway, and that could help."

"Do you think Kelly's would have an opening for me too? I could work a few hours after school a couple of days a week, and then I could pay for part of the sessions too."

"I'll ask."

Justine went to bed that night, after calling three of her closest friends, with thoughts and plans whispering in her head. She tossed and turned with excitement. Someday, she and Kerry were going to be stars.

4

Kerry leaned over her desk, humming a few notes, then writing them down. Each note had to be perfect, although her first draft, done in pencil, wasn't very neat. She didn't fill in all the notes precisely, or get them exactly centered where they belonged. That came later, after she was sure she had copied the tune right.

Justine lay across Kerry's bed, chewing on the end of a pencil. Every once in a while, she would write a few words, then stop to examine the whole piece. "Listen to this, Kerry."

"Shhh. Wait a sec. I don't want to forget this."

Justine kept writing and looking, Kerry humming and penciling. "Okay," Kerry said. "Let's hear it."

Justine grabbed the guitar and strummed a few bars and sang her new song.

"Pretty good. What about changing the second line to. . . ."

Kerry's smooth voice filled the room. How could something she sang *not* sound good?

"Okay, I like that. Say it more slowly." Justine wrote as Kerry dictated.

"And the chorus needs to be a bit more picked up, don't you think?"

"Yeah. I didn't like exactly how it came out. But I knew you could help."

Justine stood up and stretched. "Santa gave Joey a Cabbage Patch Kid for Christmas."

Kerry looked confused. "What does that have to do with writing songs?"

"Nothing," Justine replied. "I'm just worried because he likes it so much. Do you think the kid will grow up demented or something?"

Resting her chin on her hand, Kerry said, "I don't know. If I had a kid brother, I think I'd only let him play with cars."

"We aren't very liberated, are we?"

"No, probably not at all."

Walking over to Kerry's calendar, Justine touched the eleventh of January, circled in red. "What's that for?"

"That's Jack's and my third-month anniversary."

Justine shook her head. "You got lucky, didn't you, Kerry?"

"I sure did." *But I don't deserve to be loved like this*, she thought.

Justine plopped back down on the bed. Kerry turned back to her music.

The girls worked all afternoon on the new songs. Kerry wanted to get three new songs to sing for her mom's Delta

Chi meeting in five weeks. The women had decided they couldn't get any other free entertainment for their luncheon, so they might as well risk a few minutes on a member's child.

"Mom wants us to sing a few songs from *The Sound of Music* too. She says all her friends love that movie and would like the songs no matter what we sound like."

"Thanks a lot."

"That's what I told her, but I didn't mind too much. They are my favorite songs."

"Favorites because they are good songs, or favorites because of the memories they bring back?"

"I think both."

Justine giggled. "Remember how we hated each other when you first moved in?"

"How could I forget? You threw a sour orange at me from your tree."

"Well you were so weird, always in some corner deep in thought or in a book. Or listening to music," Justine added. "I wanted to run, and skate, and ride bikes. But no, you had to stay in the house."

"I can't believe it took us two years to figure out we both loved to sing."

Justine rolled over on her back. "Maybe we would never have figured it out if we didn't both get a *Sound of Music* album for Christmas."

Kerry put her feet on the chair, drawing her knees up underneath her chin. "I've often wondered if our parents got together on that. You know, they hated to see us fighting, so they bought something to bring us together."

"You goose. Don't you remember they rereleased the movie that Christmas season? Your mother took us both to see it, and we loved it so much, we acted out parts of the movie for months!"

Kerry's eyes took on a faraway look. "That was such a fun time."

"It was fun to spend all those hours harmonizing, and trying to sound Austrian."

Kerry laughed. "I'm glad the church let us sing a couple of songs for the Fellowship Feast. That cemented it forever for me, that my voice was destined to make people smile."

Rolling her eyes, Justine teased, "Aren't you getting a little carried away, here?"

Kerry stuck her tongue out at Justine. "Just because I know the course of my life, and you don't have the foggiest notion where you're headed . . ."

"Sure I know where I'm headed. I'm headed right behind you. But if you fall, I'm bailing out."

"Some friend you are."

Justine laughed. "After I help to pick you up, of course."

"Sure thing, Justine, sure thing."

With a startled, "Oh!" Justine jumped up, grabbed the pencil and paper, and began writing furiously. Kerry smiled, and turned away to her own work. She loved the creative process. How it hit you with a bang, and as you wrote, you knew it was good. As the tune came, you knew it was close to being perfect.

When the bang hit her, Kerry felt for all the world as if she had a purpose in life, a reason for being in the world Most of the time she felt so useless, taking up space for no reason.

Oh! How furious Justine got whenever Kerry suggested that she, Kerry Reynolds, might possibly be taking up useless space. "No one," Justine had shouted, "is useless in this world. God created everyone with a purpose, even if it's only to be happy, like the little kids who will be little kids forever. Don't you ever let me hear you say that again!"

"Yes, ma'am," Kerry mocked.

"And another thing," Justine said. "God doesn't do anything stupid, and He made you, didn't He?"

Embarrassed, Kerry fought back with ugly words she wished she could have stuffed right back into her mouth when she said them. "Then why do you complain about how you look all the time? So you aren't gorgeous . . . no one is gorgeous. So what if you're plain? There's nothing wrong with being plain."

Pain showed in Justine's expressive face. "So I'm plain, huh? I always complained about not being gorgeous because I only hoped that someone would agree that I wasn't gorgeous, but I was at least pretty. Thanks for setting me straight, Kerry."

Justine walked quietly through the door, then slammed it behind her. Kerry had thought she lost her best and only friend in the whole world. Later that night, Justine called her on the phone. "I don't hate you, Kerry," she said softly.

Hesitating, Kerry asked, "Are we still friends?"

Justine's loud, *"What? Are you crazy?"* sent a shiver up Kerry's spine, chilling her frightened heart. "I was mad, okay? Friends shouldn't be that honest. And when I get mad, the world knows about it. But you're my friend, and I don't let friends off that easy."

Fear left Kerry, hand in hand with the guilt, and her heart smiled.

Justine's pencil scratching stopped, halting Kerry's muse. Kerry watched Justine chew on the end of the pencil, cringing at all the bugs that must be crawling into Justine's mouth.

The front door clicked. "Mom?" Kerry called out. There was no answer. Justine looked up, her eyes glazed with creative energy. She looked back at the paper, and began to write again.

"Mom?" Kerry called again. Her bedroom door opened, and a head poked through. "Hi, honey. Hi, Justine."

Without looking up, Justine waved her hand at Mrs. Reynolds.

Mrs. Reynolds smiled, her mouth stretched into a stiff line. "More songs, girls?"

Staring at her mom, Kerry forced a cheery, "Yeah, for your Delta Chi luncheon."

The smile had already disappeared from Mrs. Reynolds' pretty face. "Oh, how nice," she said mechanically, and shut the door.

The creative spell broken, Justine looked up. "What's with her?"

Kerry put her pencil down. "Justine, I'm a little worried."

"Why?"

"Mom and Dad keep having these private meetings in the bedroom. I can hear them talking in angry whispers. Mom has been crying a lot. She denies it, but her eyes are sometimes so red and puffy, you can't tell if she has makeup on or not."

Standing up, Kerry walked to her window. She peered through the blinds to the side yard. The cement block wall looked cold and ugly—like she felt inside lately. Justine watched her, waiting for her to continue. "You saw her just now. She's not her bright self."

Justine nodded. "I've always noticed how you and your mom are so much alike. The bounce in your walk, the ability to talk with anyone, the same crystal blue eyes. Even the way you talk and think seems to be the same."

Turning her head to look at Justine, Kerry made a feeble attempt at teasing her. "Thanks, Justine. Just what I wanted to hear . . . that I'm like my *mother*."

Justine thought a moment, ignoring Kerry's tease. "You don't think they'd get a divorce, do you?"

Kerry shuddered. "I didn't think of that. But I don't think so."

Justine walked over to Kerry. A shelf with knickknacks

hung on the wall next to the window. Dusty memories placed side by side, looking like clutter to anyone else. Justine picked up her favorite, a ballerina made out of china. Her lacy tutu caught the dust, making it look a dull gray rather than white. But the detail on the face made her look again and again. It seemed almost real, as if she would talk at any moment.

Kerry spoke. "Would you think I was crazy if I told you something?"

Justine honored the softness in her tone, not coming back with something silly, as she normally would have. "I never think you're crazy, Kerry." Justine touched the tiny ballerina's feet, the toe shoes tied up around the slender ankles.

"That's my favorite thing. My very favorite. My grandmother gave it to me before she died. It was hers when she was a little girl."

Justine had heard the story before, but something in Kerry's eyes, which stared out the window, silenced her.

"Her name is Emma. I named her that."

"That hardly qualifies you for crazy status."

Kerry shook her head. "That's not the crazy part. I. . . ."

She turned and took Emma from Justine. Her face looked soft and tender, just like her mother's had when her mother had bandaged many a scraped knee when they were little kids. Kerry sighed. "I talk to her, Justine. I told her about Jack. I talk to her about you, and what we do." She set Emma on the shelf and walked back to the desk, and sat in the chair. "Crazy, huh?"

Justine picked up Emma, and sat on the bed. "Emma," she said, looking at the ballerina, "you are lucky to have such a nice friend. I am too." She looked at Kerry and smiled. "No, you're not crazy."

"Ever notice how Emma looks like me?"

"How could I not notice? I couldn't believe it when I first

saw her. I was, what, in the fifth grade? I thought it was spooky. She even has your freckles. . . ."

"And my fat thighs. . . ."

"All dancers have fat thighs. It's called *muscle*," she said, imitating Mister Rogers. "Can you say *muscle*, boys and girls? *Muscle* comes from exercise. Everybody say *exercise*. Now everyone stand up, and we'll do an exercise."

Kerry held her sides as she laughed, tears streaming down her face. "What do you do, watch him every day?"

"No, but I hear him every day. Joey watches him and does everything he says. It's a riot."

"Remember the day I was over and Mister Rogers' fish died? I don't think I have ever seen you laugh so hard in my whole life."

"And poor Joey was crying." Justine shook her head. "My mom really let me have it that night. I had to apologize to Joey."

"What a scream!"

"Yeah, and you should have seen me trying not to laugh as I apologized." Justine glanced at the clock by the side of the bed. "Oh, no, it's that time again. I'd better run, or Mom's going to ground me for three days again for coming in late."

"Maybe she just doesn't want you to miss Mister Rogers."

Laughing, Justine put Emma back on the shelf. "She always did want me to get a good education."

Kerry saw Justine out the front door, and returned to her room. It was too quiet without Justine there. Her mom made scuttering noises in her bedroom. She hated those noises. They were too mysterious. Her mother had started keeping the bedroom door locked when she was gone. It made Kerry feel like a thief.

She pulled her History book from underneath the stack of papers. She opened to chapter 7 and began to read. At the end of the chapter, she answered the questions, wondering if she'd remember the answers in the morning. The only thing that seemed to stick in her head was music. Without her music, she'd have nothing. She'd be dead inside. Dead, dead, dead, like the rotting bird she saw on the way to school. She hated death. But still, it fascinated her.

Her Biology teacher suggested she look into becoming a coroner, because of her interest in looking at dead things. She cringed at the thought.

The scuttering noises continued in her mom's room. At five, she decided she'd better remind her mom of the time. Her dad hated to come home and have dinner not even started yet. He'd been mad a lot lately.

When Kerry knocked on her mother's door, the scuttering stopped. "What?" asked a muffled voice.

"Mom, it's five. Dad will be home pretty soon."

Silence.

"Mom?"

"Will you start dinner?"

"What do you want me to fix?"

"Oh, whatever you want. Open a can of soup."

Kerry sighed. She wished she knew what was happening in this house. A curtain, somewhere, was closing. A performance was coming to an end. But what performance? Was there a next act?

In the kitchen, she peeled potatoes into a sink scarred with pot marks. Her mother hated pot marks. But she didn't seem to care about much of anything anymore.

She put the potatoes in a pot of salted water on the stove. She turned the gas flame on high.

In the refrigerator, she found a pound of hamburger. She grabbed an onion and a couple of eggs. In the near-empty freezer, she found a box of spinach. She turned up her nose and pulled it out anyway.

While the spinach thawed in the microwave, she

browned the hamburger and onion together. She took a moment out to put a Shelly Grammercy tape in the stereo. She cranked it up loud, and returned to the kitchen.

She sang every song with Shelly, practicing her harmonizing skills, and working on the high notes.

She turned the potatoes down as the water boiled over the side. Her thoughts boiled over too. They were being stirred around her brain as fast as she stirred the meat and onion.

Some days she hated being an only child. She hated having all the responsibility put on her when Mom decided to back out. She hated having no one to talk to, or share frustrations about Mom and Dad. She loved having her own room, her own music, and no little brother to sneak her tapes away and ruin them. No one to be vindictive, no one to write on her homework.

As she took the spinach from the microwave, the front door opened. "Hey," her father shouted. "Something smells great!"

"Hi, Dad!" Kerry called, trying to sound cheery.

Her father hugged her, and kissed her cheek. His brows pulled together. "Where's your mother?"

"In the bedroom."

He nodded, knowingly. Kerry wished he'd let her in on the secret. She bit her bottom lip as she added the spinach and two eggs to the hamburger. "Dad?"

"Umm hmm?" he muttered as he flipped through the stack of mail.

She took a deep breath and continued. "What's going on around here?"

She noticed a slight change in his face. She couldn't quite detect what it was. "Oh, nothing. Hey, I'd better give your mother her hello kiss." He dropped the mail on the table and fled.

Dinner was as it had been for the past week. No more

delightful chatting. *It's too quiet*, Kerry thought. *Dad used to be so happy to share about the people he saw and met, the progress they'd made on the most recent building project. Mom and I laughing over some silly thing, usually how Dad got his tongue tied and said something wrong.*

Her father broke into her thoughts. "Kerry, this is great stuff! We ought to have it more often."

Kerry smiled, "Thanks, Dad." Her mom had taken off to some other planet. She ate, picking up tiny pieces of food.

Mr. Reynolds looked at his wife with concern. "Eloise?"

Kerry's mom looked up, like a surprised bird. "Harold?"

"Isn't this a great dinner?"

Her eyes lost a little of the fog. "Oh, yes. Thanks, Kerry." She turned to Mr. Reynolds. "Harold, Kerry has been such a help to me lately. I don't know what I'd do without her."

Kerry should have felt a warm glow over her mother's praise. But she didn't. Something was missing. It seemed phony. She looked at both of them, lost in their own thoughts. She had to know, she had to ask. She looked at her plate, picking apart a piece of spinach. She lifted it, and sighed.

"Mom? Dad? I have something to ask you."

Both heads turned to her, expectant.

"Things have been so weird around here lately. I . . . I, uh, I wondered if you're getting a divorce." There, it was out.

Her mom and dad looked at each other. Kerry didn't like the look. It said too much she wasn't supposed to know. It said there was a secret there she could not be a part of. It said something scary was about to happen to her family.

Her mother's head turned back to look at Kerry. "Why no, dear, we're not getting a divorce. What ever gave you that idea?"

Her voice is too mechanical, Kerry thought. "Well," she said, feeling stupid for bringing it up, and at the same time, knowing. . . . "You and Dad have been fighting a lot. And you cry, and lock the bedroom, and do mysterious things in there."

Her dad forced a smile. "I suppose you have seen those things. But honey, parents sometimes have problems they have to work out themselves. It's not terrible. It's not a divorce." He stood up and massaged her shoulders, giving a little laugh. "Mom and I have been together too long to get a divorce, haven't we dear?"

As Mrs. Reynolds looked at him, a tiny but genuine smile broke through. "Yes dear, that we have."

Kerry didn't know what to think. Her dad's words sounded true enough. But that look. What did that look mean?

❧ 5 ❧

❧ The next morning, Kerry felt stupid for asking her parents if they were getting a divorce. Of all the idiot ideas! So what if her mother was sad? Her mother overreacted a lot about so many things. And once a month, she knew she'd better steer clear.

She focused her attention on the bright, clear morning. "No smog today," Jack commented brightly.

"It's Rose Bowl weather," she added.

She liked being around Jack. His sense of humor surprised her at times. He seemed to know when to lighten a heavy situation, or stop a lighthearted one from getting carried away.

As they walked together down the hall, Kerry loved the

looks that came their way. The guys would wink at Jack, with an approving glance at Kerry. Some even gave him the okay sign when they thought she couldn't see.

It pleased her that these looks didn't seem to affect Jack. He didn't seem to gloat over being with her. She liked that.

Kerry's friends all said hello, with a bit of a lift to the word. She knew the message. She said it herself when she saw one of her friends with a popular or good-looking guy. It was an acknowledging message: "I see you and are you ever lucky." *Amazing*, Kerry thought, *what one word can say.*

"Are you always this deep in thought?" Jack asked. "Or am I so terribly boring that you have to pretend to be so you don't offend me?"

Kerry laughed, tossing her head back. "My dad says I 'ponder' too much. So I guess I do think a lot. I always thought it was normal to think hard about everything, but I've found out it's not."

"I wouldn't say it's abnormal either. It's just not the way everybody operates."

"Maybe not, but sometimes I feel like there's something wrong with me for being such a thinker."

Jack looked at her, amused. "If there is something wrong with you, then there's something wrong with me. I'm a thinker too."

"You know, I told Justine you understand my ponderings. You've never really said so, but I could just tell."

Jack pulled her close. "Of course I understand. Two thinkers understand each other." He looked at her, his eyes saying even more than his words.

"Here's my class," Kerry said, disappointed she had to stop the conversation.

"See you at lunch," Jack said, touching her elbow before he left.

Kerry could hardly concentrate on her History. It all seemed so boring when real life was happening right then and there. Real life that promised to give her a guy who was more than all the flakes she had dated in the past. All they seemed to talk about were themselves. At school they were kids, but when they took her out, they took on a different air. She felt like they were trying to be her father, rather than her friend.

Sometimes they told her things with a voice of authority. When they touched her, she felt the same wonderful warmth and yummy sensations as she did with Jack. But those feelings wore off after a couple of dates. Then she couldn't stand to have them touch her. They acted as if she were privileged to have them kiss her.

So she never dated anyone more than a few times. Sometimes she only went out to have something to do. She had always longed for someone like Jack, who could carry on a conversation and still be a friend. Now that she had him, she feared someday he would wake up and see her for who she really was, and not like her anymore.

A paper fluttered to her desk as the class moaned in unison. The teacher raised a map, revealing a list of questions. *Pop quiz! Yuck. And today of all days.*

***

The next Wednesday, Claudia handed Kerry a slip of paper with two addresses on it. "Now, Kerry, are you sure you aren't rushing into this?"

Kerry stood on one foot, then the other. "You said I've improved so much. And Justine and I really think we can put together a terrific demo tape."

Claudia sat on her piano bench. She pulled off her stack of bracelets, setting them on the edge of the piano. Her long slender fingers swept back her hair. "It costs lots of money. There's an awful lot of rejection in this business. Can you take it?"

Kerry smiled. "I've already sent off two tapes to all the

Artist and Repertoire people of every major record company I could find. I've gotten three rejection letters. It isn't bad. I even bought a corkboard to post them on. I also listen to your criticism without falling apart, don't I?"

Claudia cringed. "Oh, Kerry. Don't post your rejection letters! Throw them away. Keep track of who has turned the song down, but don't post them."

"It's okay, Claudia."

Shaking her head, Claudia reached out her hands. "Sending a tape to promote an original song is one thing, but the cost in developing a good quality demo tape to promote yourself as a singer, is quite another."

"My dad said to get him the prices, and he'll decide." Kerry bounced around the room a little, unable to hold still. "They're going to like us, I know they will."

"I hope you can take all the disappointment and waiting that goes with the business." Claudia sighed. "I've given you the names and addresses of two reputable, but fairly inexpensive, eight-track studios. You will have to call for the prices. Now let's work."

Kerry raced home to the phone, calling the first studio on her list. The Beverly Arts Recording Studio charged an hourly rate of thirty dollars. A piano player would cost her sixty dollars for the song, a violinist would cost seventy dollars for the song. A flutist, the same as the piano. If she wanted drums and a bass guitar, that would be another hundred. It would take at least five studio hours to record one song, he told her.

Kerry added it all up on a piece of paper, horrified at the cost of doing a four-song demo tape. Over sixteen hundred dollars! And that was if everything went well. Add to that, the cost of black-and-white glossies to send out with the tape.

She called the other studio, but they charged even more.

Her father had told her he could maybe get five hundred set aside. It was hopeless.

She crumpled her figures and shoved them in the wastebasket. Tears came to her eyes, and she wiped them away with two quick, angry moves. *Don't cry, idiot. I'll just have to concentrate on selling my songs.*

She leaned over and held her stomach. The pain passed after a few minutes. She opened her drawer and unwrapped the cellophane from three Maalox tablets. Two no longer worked.

She shoved her disappointment into a closet in her mind. She was so tired of being unhappy. She had a wonderful boyfriend . . . a wonderful friend, and lots of other nice friends at school. She should be happy. Everyone told her often enough how lucky she was. So why did she feel herself slipping into a black hole?

She hated herself for feeling her mom cared more for her friend Sally than her. Her dad cared more for work, but that was expected of men. She picked up Emma and twirled her around. "Grandma loved me, didn't she Emma? But she's not around to love me anymore."

She wondered if her mom ever kept a diary and what she would say about Kerry in it. Maybe she'd write that Kerry was never meant to be. *Why didn't you have more children? Because I was so awful? Or because you never wanted children in the first place? Me, a mistake.*

Kerry crawled under her bed, and lay there looking at the crossboards and fraying fabric. She wrinkled her dust-filled nose. She started to giggle, remembering how many times she had crawled under her bed as a kid. It seemed safe under there during the day, even though monsters lived there at night. She used to lie there and pick at the under fabric, and draw pictures on the boards. The pictures were there now, but she couldn't figure out what they had been.

She found one barely recognizable picture of Emma. She

knew it was her, because she remembered the day she had drawn it. She had just gotten back from Grandma's where she had fallen in love with Emma. She came back to draw a picture of her, where she could lie and dream of being like the beautiful dancer.

She didn't have long to dream, for her grandmother gave her Emma on her next birthday. After that, she didn't crawl under the bed again, until now.

The phone rang. She bumped her head getting out from underneath the bed. "Hello?" she said with a giggle.

"Hi, it's me," Justine said. "I wondered if you found out about the demo tape stuff."

Kerry blew a raspberry into the phone. "You can't believe how much those guys charge! I'd have to be rich to record a demo tape."

"How much?"

"Over sixteen hundred."

Justine let out a long, low, "Wow."

"You ain't kiddin'. I guess we'll have to stick to the song selling."

"That's it!" Justine shouted into Kerry's ear. "We'll sell a song, and make enough money to cut the demo tape. Let's put 'Oh for the Joy' on tape, and send it out too."

"Great idea."

Kerry hung up the phone, hope showing through the clouds of disappointment.

6

Justine loved seeing Jack and Kerry together. Something in Kerry's face lit up and glowed. Jack was no different. Tall and lanky, his black hair always in place, he lost his clumsy look when he walked with Kerry. He seemed at ease and comfortable. They were quite the odd couple. Some of the tall girls complained, because they felt the short girls should date the short guys.

When Jack bent down to kiss Kerry, it was like an adult drinking from a child-size water fountain. Cute, awkward.

Justine opened her locker with a few quick spins of the combination lock. The black dial swirled around. The door vibrated as she yanked it open, adding to the tune the other lockers made. *An orchestra of metal,* Justine thought. She imagined a DJ's voice sounding off in her head. "We were the first station to bring you the sounds of heavy metal, and we will now be the first to bring you the sounds of light metal. From the halls of Central High. . . ."

Kerry's voice interrupted her silly thoughts. "Justine," she said happily, "we got another rejection yesterday."

"Oh, phooey. From who?"

"CBS."

"Why do you sound so happy?"

Kerry shrugged, Jack towering over her. "I guess I know someday, somewhere, someone will see our talent. I'm not worried."

Justine looked at Jack. "How can she be so cool? How can she always let things run off her back like this?"

Jack smiled. "That's my Kerry. Nothing much bothers her. We had to wait two hours in Westwood to see that new Sally Field movie, because we just missed getting into the show before. You know how long those lines are . . . we took a chance and didn't make it. And you know what she said?"

"No, what?" asked Justine, watching Kerry adore Jack.

"She said it was great, because that gave us two hours to talk some more. That's one of the things I like so much about her. Other girls would have cried, or thrown a little girl's fit."

"Like I'm going to do right now," Justine said. "I'm ticked that those stupid idiots at CBS can't see talent when it comes knocking at their door. Blind fools. Now that just ruins my day."

Kerry smiled, "Oh, Justine. You'll be out of your snit by third period. You watch."

Justine couldn't help but smile. She slammed her locker on her sweater and rolled her eyes. "See? I'm destined for a rotten day. See you two later."

Walking to History, Justine wished for all the world she

could react like Kerry—to let few things bother her. Seeing Kerry worried about her mother was practically the only time she'd ever seen Kerry truly upset. She had her moments, brief, fleeting moments, when you could see the anger, or sadness. But it never lasted for long.

Justine wondered if it had anything to do with Kerry's faith. Justine believed in God, loved Him and all, but she got mad at Him and doubted half the things He did or didn't do. Kerry never seemed to doubt.

***

At lunch, Justine decided to make herself scarce. Jack and Kerry were mooning over each other, and Justine didn't feel like trying to break the spell with some inane conversation. She wandered from group to group, half listening to the conversations. The drugheads talked in long low tones about their drugs and drug parties. Those who had split into pairs, hung all over each other, making out, oblivious to the rest of the group.

The flits, the girls her grandmother called "easy," giggled together. Most sat on tables, their tight skirts high on their legs. As they talked to each other, they never looked at one another. They watched for the guys. It sounded like a construction site when the best-looking guys walked by. The girls whistled and waved.

Chuckling, Justine thought of how naive Kerry thought they were just friendly, and a bit overpainted.

She wandered into the grove, where four eucalyptus trees shaded three picnic tables. The grove belonged to the regs. The regs were the regular kids, named so by the drugheads and the flits. The nerds named no one, living out their lives socializing with each other and their books.

"Hey, it's Justine!" called Cathy. The group turned as one herd, all smiling. "All right, it's the song of the party."

Justine smiled as she threw her sweater across one of the

tables. "Hi, folks! Anything exciting happen today?" Justine asked. She had friends in every group. She could get along with anybody as long as they were basically human.

Most of her friends hung out in the grove. She spent time with each, depending on her mood. If she felt like laughing, she teased with Pete, Larry, and Sue.

If she felt like talking over nothing in particular, she leaned more toward Eileen, Beth, and Cathy, who was permanently attached to Frank.

"Not much is happening around here, that's for sure," Larry answered.

"Where's Kerry?" asked Cathy. "I've got to ask her for some help on this horrid music homework."

"She and Jack are in their own little world. I don't think she'd be of much help to anyone right now."

Cathy looped her little finger with Frank's. "I know how she feels." She looked at Frank, giving him a special smile, then kissed his cheek.

"Don't your glasses ever get steamed up?" teased Pete.

"At least they don't both have braces," added Eileen.

Sitting next to Larry, Justine pulled out her lunch sack. Larry looked at her, and then at her lunch. "Got anything worth eating?"

"Nothing to share, Larry."

She opened her sack, feeling funny that Larry kept staring at her. She wondered why his hands trembled. Larry, so sure of himself, could be terribly obnoxious at times.

"Uhh, Justine?" he asked so quietly, Justine wondered if he had really spoken.

She looked at him. His head hung down, his hands folded like a church boy. "Would you go with me to see the new Dudley Moore movie on Saturday night? Jack asked me if I wanted to go, and I thought maybe, since you are Kerry's friend, that you would like to go too."

"Larry, don't feel obligated to ask me to go, just because

I'm Kerry's friend, okay? Ask who you really want to go with."

Larry blushed. "I didn't mean for it to sound like that, Justine. I really do want to go with you."

Justine tried to smile, but her sandwich filled her mouth. She nodded instead.

"You mean you'll go?"

Justine swallowed. "Yes, Larry, I'll go. I'd enjoy that very much."

Cathy stood in front of Frank, who sat on the table. She had her back to Justine. As Justine finished her answer, Cathy turned her head and winked . Justine dropped her eyes, afraid she'd laugh.

***

Saturday morning, Justine wished she hadn't agreed to wrap packages at Kelly's. It would be so much nicer to sleep all day. She pulled her covers over her head to shut out the sun. Dark and warmth encouraged her to go back to sleep. She wondered what it would be like to be in love. To have someone care for her. A hunk with blond hair and blue eyes came into her dream. He stared in a mirror as he talked with her. She decided he cared too much for himself. As hard as she tried, she couldn't imagine what being in love was like.

She only knew what it was like to be on a date, with nice guys, as well as jerks. She sighed and gave up the dream.

A knocking on her door startled her. "Justine, get up!" her mom encouraged. "It's your first day of work, remember?"

Justine pulled the covers down under her chin. "Yeah, I remember."

Her mom opened the door. She put her hands on her pink-robed waist. "Now, Justine," she said kindly. "I thought you wanted this job."

Justine sat up and stretched her hands over her head. "I do, Mom. I just wish it weren't on Saturday mornings."

"You'll get used to it. I think you'll like it there."

"Do you?"

Mrs. Crawford sat on the edge of Justine's bed, tucking her feet underneath her robe. "It took me a couple of days feeling like I had no business being there. But then I liked it."

"Why didn't you think you belonged?"

"I guess because it has been so long since I've been anything but a housewife. All the people are so efficient at what they do. I stumbled over everything. I thought I'd never learn how to work that computer register. The last register I used was more simple."

"But you like it now?"

Mrs. Crawford nodded. "It's nice to be around pretty things all day, to talk with other adults, to help people. Silly how something so minor can make you feel so good about yourself."

Justine laughed. "All I want to do is be able to make money and not be bored stiff while I'm doing it."

A smile played in the corner of Mrs. Crawford's mouth. "Oh, Justine. When are you ever going to grow up?"

"Maybe next year, Mom. I'm having too much fun being a kid."

"Enjoy it all you can. Growing up isn't always fun."

"Neither is working."

"Justine, you'll have fun wrapping gifts there. I'll guarantee it." Mrs. Crawford stood up, pushing back her graying hair. "But you'll never find out unless you get yourself out of that warm bed and into the shower."

"Yes ma'am," Justine said, jumping out of bed and saluting. Mrs. Crawford left the room, shaking her head and chuckling.

At five minutes to ten, Mrs. Crawford drove into Kelly's

parking lot. She touched Justine lightly on the hand, and looked her in the eye. "Justine, you'll do fine. Just do your best and don't fool around. Mr. Kelly seems frightening, but he is simply all business. He wants things done a certain way, and that's his right. He will let you know when you've done a good job."

Justine bit her bottom lip. "Thanks, Mom."

"I'll pick you up at three."

Justine knocked on the locked door. A woman came to the door, peered out the window, and shook her head. She pointed to the posted hours sign and walked away.

Justine rolled her eyes. She knocked again, and the same woman came to the door. She held five fingers in front of her agitated face. Justine knocked again and as the woman turned her back, she called out, "I work here."

The woman looked confused. A man came behind her, looked out the window, and unlocked the door. "Thank you, Mr. Kelly," Justine said as the woman babbled angry words about pesky customers.

Mr. Kelly turned to the woman and said, "Mrs. Wesperton, I would like you to meet Miss Crawford, our new gift-wrapping girl."

Mrs. Wesperton turned beet red. Justine tried to be polite and hold her laughter inside. "Nice to meet you," Justine said, holding out her hand.

Mrs. Wesperton sputtered and turned away, muttering as she went.

It was as if Mr. Kelly hadn't noticed a thing. He said in a kind, firm voice, "Follow me, Miss Crawford." He led her to the back of the store, to a small booth. He unlocked the door and began to point out things and give directions. Justine tried to keep her mind on what he was saying.

"If you have any questions, you may speak to me or Mrs. Wesperton." He looked down and cleared his throat. Justine could have sworn he was trying not to laugh. "But the best person to speak to would be Mrs. Riley. She knows more about this store than anyone."

Justine stood in her small booth, touching each wrapping paper, trying to decide what each should be used for.

The rest of the day passed, boring and busy. She wasted so much paper, she wondered if she'd ever be asked back. She never seemed to get the right amount of paper pulled off the roll. It was either too much or too little. By three, she was ready to go home and sleep.

7

Justine leaned on the window edge of Kerry's car. "Does my mom know you're here?"

"Yep. I asked her if you could go shopping with me this afternoon. She said fine. Want to?"

Justine closed her eyes a minute, thinking of how nice a nap would feel. When her eyes popped open, she said, "Sure!" She ran around the other side of the car, and slid in. She kicked off her shoes and rubbed her feet. "I'm not used to standing on my feet all day. I was ready to go home and take a nap."

"You don't have to go shopping with me, you know."

Justine stared at Kerry. "I know." She waited until the light turned green, then asked, "Where are we going?"

"To Musicland."

"I should have known."

"We can go to Clothes Line too, if you want."

"Of course I want to. I only wish I had my first paycheck. I don't get paid until next week."

Confused, Kerry said, "I thought you were going to use that money for voice lessons."

"Part of it. Part of it must go to clothes. I mean, who in their right mind would make money and not spend any of it on clothes?"

Kerry sighed. "Probably me. I would rather buy music."

Justine stretched her long legs out the best she could. "I wish you weren't so short, or that this car had a split seat. My legs are killing me."

"Sorry. Maybe I shouldn't have chosen a long-legged person for a friend."

Justine stuck her tongue out at her. "What are you going to buy today?"

"I'm not sure. I want to get some varied types of music to sing along with. I need to be more versatile in my style."

Justine cringed. "You won't get any opera, will you?"

Kerry broke out into warbled song. Justine plugged her ears. Kerry giggled. "I don't think I want to be *that* versatile."

Walking through the mall, Justine carefully looked at all the outfits the girls wore. She took special note of the accessories. "Why can't I think of that?" she asked Kerry as she pointed toward a mannequin.

"Because you aren't a fashion designer."

"Hey, maybe that's what I should be."

Kerry rolled her eyes.

"Where's Jack?" Justine asked.

"He's doing some work for his dad."

"What kind of work is that?"

"Didn't I tell you? His dad's a History professor at Occidental College, and sometimes Jack does research for him."

"How boring, poor guy."

Kerry shook her head. "He loves it."

Stopping in front of a display window, Justine looked at the shoes. "Is he still going tonight?"

"Of course. Are you still coming with Larry?"

" 'Fraid so."

"Don't you want to?"

Justine turned away from the shoes. "Oh, I don't know. He's funny, but he's so nervous. Nervous guys always talk weird."

"He won't be nervous with Jack."

"I hope you're right. I want to have *fun* tonight!"

***

Larry came to the door, dressed in his gray Levi's and a blue shirt she wasn't sure how to describe. Wild and cute, maybe. He looked more nervous than the day he asked her out. "Ready, Justine?"

Justine looked back at her dad. "Bye, Dad."

"Bye, Jussie. See you by midnight?"

"Yes, Dad."

Larry opened the car door, and Justine slid into the car next to Pete. Kerry and Jack turned around in the front seat. As everyone said hi, Justine thought she noticed something dull about Kerry's eyes. Kerry's voice sounded cheery and normal, *but her eyes,* Justine thought. *Maybe it's just the dark.*

The movie was as funny as Justine had hoped, but Kerry didn't seem to laugh as much or as hard as anyone else. Even when they gathered around the table in the darkened pizza parlor, Justine thought she could see a difference in Kerry.

As the guys went to order the pizza and soft drinks, Justine sat down next to Kerry. "What's wrong?"

"Oh, nothing that won't be okay. Really, it is okay, it's

great. I guess it just came as a surprise, and, I. . . ." Kerry looked down and sighed. When she lifted her head, she had painted on a smile.

"So don't keep me in suspense. Are you and Jack breaking up?"

Kerry laughed. "No. I think it's a good thing between Jack and me. I don't think we'll ever break up."

Justine raised her eyebrows. She lowered her voice to a whisper. "Are you guys talking about getting married?"

"Not really."

"Okay, so what's wrong?"

"We're moving . . . to Colorado. My parents dropped the bomb on me during dinner."

Justine shook her head slowly. "No. You can't."

Kerry forced a laugh. "It's not like I have any choice."

"Why do you have to move?"

"Dad got offered a top position with the company. He'll make such good money, I can have voice lessons twice a week, and even think about doing a real demo tape."

"But where would you do all that? The best recording studios are here. And so are the voice teachers. I've never heard of a great teacher in Colorado."

Kerry looked over her shoulder. "Here come the guys."

"Does Jack know?"

Kerry shook her head.

The guys rehashed the movie, laughing again at the funny lines and situations. Kerry forced herself to laugh with them. Justine picked at her pizza.

Larry looked at her. "Justine, you were the one who wanted pizza. Now you aren't eating any. What's the deal? I paid good money for it," he teased.

"Knock it off," Kerry said.

Larry shrugged his shoulders. He put his arm around Justine. "Sorry."

"It's okay." Justine wished he'd take his arm off her. Somehow it was an ugly gesture.

At Justine's front door, Larry mashed his lips against hers. "See you on Monday."

"Sure, Larry."

Sunday morning in church, Kerry's bounce and happiness had returned. She and Justine sat in the back row in Sunday school, whispering during the songs and announcements.

"When do you move?" Justine asked.

"March fifteenth. Maybe as late as the thirtieth. It depends on our selling the house."

"That's only a month away."

"I know."

"Well, maybe no one will buy the house."

"It's across the street from the college. Of course someone will buy the house."

Justine looked down at her hands. "It's not fair, Kerry. You're my best friend. Who will I tell everything to? Who will keep me singing? Who will I sing with, write songs with?" Justine put her face into her hands and started to cry.

Putting her hand on Justine's back, Kerry encouraged, "God always has something better if He takes away something good."

Justine looked up, and wiped the tears. "I don't know if I can believe that."

Kerry leaned over. "Look, I'll leave, and a few minutes later, you leave too."

In the hallway, the girls sat on the floor. "Justine, I was beginning to get upset about this move. Then I remembered that God loves me more than you do. He knows I want to sing. He knows where I can best learn. It's okay. He wouldn't send me to Colorado if it wouldn't be good for me there." *But it's so dark and awful now,* Kerry thought. *I hurt. I hurt so bad. Maybe when I get there the hurt will go away.*

Justine sat up straight. "I know—I'll ask my mom if you can live with us. Just until the end of the school year. Then you can keep going to singing lessons with Claudia, you can go to the prom, graduate with our class, and everything."

Kerry turned her head away, a wishful look on her face. "No, Justine, I don't think that's a part of the plan." *Oh God, I wish it was.*

"How do you know?" Justine demanded.

Kerry shook her head, then pressed her fingers to her temples. She began to breathe deeply. Suddenly she looked up. "It's okay, Justine. Really it is."

Justine pushed off her shoes with her toes. "What does your mom think?"

Kerry pulled at a stray string on her dress. "That's why she's been acting so bizarre lately. She's freaking out. I really and truly don't know how she's going to survive without Sally. I don't think she knows how she's going to survive without Sally either."

Kerry hit the floor with her fist. "I'm not going to fall apart like my mother. I'm not! It's silly and foolish to cry over things you can't control or change. I'm going to do fine, you just watch. I'm not going to cry. I'll make new friends."

Justine started to cry again. "But I'll miss you."

"We'll write. And I bet we write every day."

"It's not the same."

Kerry's voice quieted. "No, it's not the same." The pain stabbed a little harder. The darkness deepened.

***

Kerry sat on her front porch, leaning against the stucco archway. Each square of the sidewalk path leading to the porch had memories for her. All the times she and Justine had played hopscotch. The times they did chalk drawings, each one declaring hers was best.

The ivy made a deep green fringe around the lawn. In it,

they lost balls for playing jacks. They found bugs and screamed at them, or smashed them.

A little brown Toyota parked at the curb. Kerry set her smile, and remembered to think of only the positive things, not the negative. Lock away the pain and it can't hurt you. Pretend it isn't there and it leaves you alone.

Jack bounded up the stairs between the ivy, his face beaming. He sat next to Kerry, leaned over, and kissed her. Kerry pulled him toward her, making the kiss last longer.

Jack looked at her, surprised. "How come the nice kiss?"

Kerry looked into eyes. "I'm going to miss you, Jack."

Tilting his head, Jack's eyes clouded over. "But I thought we had such a good relationship. . . ."

Kerry shook her head. "We do, Jack. It's not that. I'm moving to Colorado."

Jack dropped his head into his hands, slowly shaking his head. "I knew this would happen. I knew it."

"Knew what?"

"I don't know, I guess I figured that something this good couldn't last."

"It can last, Jack. We can make it last," Kerry pleaded.

Jack looked at her, holding both her hands, rubbing them with his thumbs. "Kerry, I know that right now, at this very minute, you want it to last, and so do I. But the instant those Colorado guys get a look at you, I've lost you."

Kerry laughed. "Oh, Jack, don't worry about something that's not going to happen. You think I'm pretty because you're prejudiced."

Jack shook his head. "Kerry, all my friends tell me how they think you're the cutest girl in school."

"Then why didn't any of them ever ask me out?"

"Because they were afraid you'd turn 'em down."

Kerry snorted. "I hardly believe that."

"It's true. And you'll find out at your new school."

Kerry put her arm around Jack's neck, rubbing her nose

against his. "If they ask, I'll tell them no. I've never met anyone like you, Jack. You're special. I'm holding on for that. I'll even apply to go to school out here. I'll be back."

She kissed Jack on the cheek and jumped up. "C'mon," she said, pulling on his hand. "You promised to take me ice-skating. I'm not letting you back down."

"I'm not much in the mood for that anymore. How about if we drive up around Mulholland instead?"

"Anything to be with you."

As they drove, Kerry filled Jack in on all the details. She spoke in her bubbly, happy tone, trying to convey to Jack that everything would be okay.

Jack didn't say much. He listened, heard, and did not hear. He was losing the most important person in his life. He tried to believe in the rightness of things like Kerry did. But it didn't seem right. It seemed all wrong.

8

Kerry hoped no one guessed at the deepening sadness inside of her. She laughed and smiled at the parties her friends gave to say good-bye to her. She opened the gifts, and was overwhelmed by their love for her.

She hugged them, cried with them, and played silly games with them. Each day, the sun shone in a cloudless sky, while the dark clouds formed in her heart. At school, kids she didn't know came to tell her they'd miss her music, and hoped to hear her on the radio someday.

At church, even the adults came to tell her good-bye. All this love was being heaped on her, and she couldn't soak it up. *I'm a duck, all right,* she thought. *Everything rolls off my back, even the love of friends.*

She smiled, laughed, and smiled some more—always cheerful about the move ahead. She told why she was happy about the move so many times, her mind would think about other things as she spoke.

Every time she got scared, thinking about moving to a new school, and a new town, she turned off the feelings. *It will be okay*, she told herself over and over. *I'm in God's will, so there will be nothing I can't handle. Nothing can or will go wrong in God's plan.*

She spent as much time with Jack and Justine as she could. "You guys are so glum," she told them one night as she and Jack sat on Justine's porch swing.

Justine, curled up on a lounge chair, piled her hair on top of her head. "We have to make up for you," she said pointedly. "I don't know how you can be happy about this whole thing."

Kerry sighed. "I don't want to get into it again. I swear, I've told everyone why a thousand times."

Jack shifted, and put his arm around Kerry. "And you can say it a thousand times more, and we can still disagree with you. Don't you understand how much we love you?"

"What has that got to do with it?"

Justine moaned. Jack squeezed Kerry's shoulder, answering out of frustration. "It's got everything to do with it. But since we can't seem to get through to you, you'll just have to take our word for it. We're sad because you're leaving, and you're important to us. A big happy spot will have disappeared from our lives."

Kerry's laugh sounded like tinsel. "Oh, you guys will forget me in no time. Love is all relative anyway. When the object of love is around, feelings of love abound. When the object of love is gone, the feelings of love disappear too."

Justine looked at Jack. "It's hopeless." She looked across the street, watching the college students fight with a water hose. "Are you all packed, Kerry?"

"Almost. I have to do most of everything. Mom isn't home much. She says it hurts too much to be at home. The bare walls remind her of the move, and she doesn't want to think about it."

"Talk about glum," Jack added. "That woman's got the market on that."

"No kidding," Kerry agreed. "Her doctor gave her a gigantic bottle of pills to help her calm down. She can't do anything, including sleep, without one of those pills."

"I saw that bottle," Jack said. "I couldn't believe a doctor would prescribe so many."

"It's because of the move. He thought he'd give her enough to last until she could get settled, and then go to a doctor there. That's the one thing I can say about Mom. She won't take more than she's supposed to. She's so worried about them lasting long enough."

"I can never imagine my mom taking pills like that," Justine said.

Kerry waved her hand at Justine. "Your mom is like you. You'd think her heart's going to rupture one minute, and as soon as she's blown up, everything's fine."

Jack smiled a tiny smile. "Sounds like my dad. I think I'm more even tempered. Kind of in between you two."

***

Four men scurried in and out of Kerry's house like busy mice. Sweat poured down their faces and stained their shirts. Kerry sat in the corner of the lawn, watching each piece of her life stacked in the big truck.

Justine walked around the nose of the truck, which extended into the street. She waved at Kerry as she approached. Tears poured down her face. She sat next to Kerry, not saying a word. She sniffled every so often, and wiped her face with her sweat shirt sleeve.

Jack drove up, his little car screeching as he pulled a

U-turn in front of the house. He didn't jump out the way he usually did. He sort of unfolded himself, and let the door fall shut. He hiked up through the ivy, then sat down on the other side of Kerry. His voice was low and husky as he greeted the girls. Neither of them answered, but Kerry laid her head on his shoulder.

Two hours later, Justine's tears had dried, and her sweat shirt had been pushed up to her elbows. Jack had gone to get them hamburgers. Kerry ate one bite, then put it away. Justine didn't do much better.

The men closed the door to the moving van, and locked it with a large padlock and chain. They shook hands with Mr. Reynolds, climbed into the cab, and drove away.

Mr. Reynolds approached the little group as quietly as if they were in a holy sanctuary. He bowed his head as he spoke. "Kerry, Mom is going to need you to help her clean the house. We'll need to leave no later than four."

Kerry stood, brushing off the seat of her pants. "Well?"

Justine jumped up. "I'll help, Kerry."

"Me too," Jack said.

Kerry was about to tell them they didn't have to help, but she changed her mind.

All three went into the bare house. It was a shock to see it like that. It had lost so much of what had been home. They each picked up either a rag, a roll of paper towels, or a bottle of some kind of cleaning junk, and got to work. Jack washed the windows, Justine washed the walls, while Kerry crawled around the house dusting baseboards.

Next they tackled the bathroom and kitchen. Mrs. Reynolds vacuumed the same rooms, over and over.

They finished at three. They looked at each other. The minutes hurt. Thoughts hurt. Jack cried, his eyes filling up slowly with tears. Each one dripped down his face. He hugged Kerry so tight, she didn't know if she could breathe. But she didn't care. He kissed the top of her head, and lay his cheek on her hair. They kissed once. The longest, softest kiss Kerry had ever had. Its taste was salty and full of loneliness and sorrow.

Justine hugged her too. She wanted to kiss her cheek, but was embarrassed, and didn't.

Kerry's patient dad leaned out the car window, his gentle voice urging, "Kerry, honey. We've got to go now."

Justine could have sworn she saw tears in Mr. Reynolds' eyes. She figured she must be mistaken. *What reason would he have to cry? He's not leaving his best friend behind.*

Mrs. Reynolds stared out the front window, never looking to either side. Kerry's arm waved and waved out the back window until they couldn't see her anymore.

***

Kerry looked out the window, watching memories pass. She felt a tugging inside her chest. She saw herself—a little kid pulling a wagon load of tears and fear. She shook her head, angry at herself for wanting to fall apart. She forced herself to look ahead, at the future, at her new life in a strange and wonderful land.

But I don't want to go.

Colorado is gorgeous. There are lots of kids there, lots of new friends.

I want Jack. I want Justine.

You can't, so you might as well look on the bright side.

Kerry looked out the window, and tried to find it, as they headed away from the setting sun.

***

The next morning, after a stomach-churning breakfast at Denny's, Kerry realized her mom must have taken one of her pills. She was bright and happy, more cheerful than Kerry had seen her in months.

Her dad seemed neither happy nor sad. He was very quiet, though, so unusual for him.

"So," Mrs. Reynolds said brightly. "We're on our way to a new adventure, huh, Kerry?"

"Sure."

"You don't sound so sure about it."

"I'm trying, Mom. Maybe it will take me a little bit of time."

"Not too much, I hope. Sullenness isn't attractive, you know."

Kerry chewed on her tongue, so she wouldn't sass back. "I know." *I guess it's different when you're sullen, huh, Mom?*

Mrs. Reynolds twisted around in her seat, resting her chin on the back of it. "You and Justine did a terrific job at the Delta Chi lunch. I'm telling you, Kerry. You guys are dynamite together. I had so many ladies come up to me afterward and say what a gorgeous voice you have."

Kerry's face lit up. *"Really, Mom?"*

Mrs. Reynolds nodded. "The president said if we weren't moving, she would have asked you back for the high celebration in June. That's the biggest event of the year, with families invited and everything."

"I know, Mom. I've been before."

"Oh, that's right. Anyway, I couldn't have been more proud."

"I wish you had told me earlier so I could have told Justine. We both wondered how we did."

Mrs. Reynolds turned to face front, sighing. "I'm sorry, Kerry. I was feeling a little sad that day. Just knowing it would be my last meeting. . . ."

Mr. Reynolds put his hand on hers. "There's an organization like Delta Chi near our new home. You might enjoy that."

The pleasant look left Mrs. Reynolds' face as she looked at him a moment. "Yes, dear," she said.

Something slipped inside Kerry. She tried to grab it, but missed. Like the time she and Daddy had gone fishing from a rowboat. She lost hold of the oar, and it slipped into the water, just out of reach. They laughed until their sides hurt as they tried to grasp that stupid oar. But it floated quietly away, always a hand's length too far.

Oh, how they laughed.

Kerry didn't laugh now. Things were dying all around her, and she couldn't stop it. Every mile, every tumbleweed, every rock they passed stuck inside her. She stared at the back of her father's head, noticing how the hairs clumped together. And she forgot about dying things.

❦ 9 ❧

❦Kerry had the feeling they were in Los Angeles again, a cold Los Angeles. The mountains were far more majestic, but still, she hadn't expected such a large city. She wasn't real sure what she had expected.

The moving men sat in their truck, drinking coffee from a steaming thermos. "Sorry we're late," Mr. Reynolds called to them.

"No problem," called the driver, obviously not meaning it.

Kerry wandered around the apartment, wondering how their furniture would all fit. They hadn't lived in an apartment since before they moved up the street from Justine. She didn't remember much about it, except she couldn't go out and play when she wanted. There was no grass.

Kerry unpacked each box as the movers brought them into her room. She wanted to cry as she unpacked all the things that reminded her of home, and friends. But the tears had dried up.

When the movers finished leaving their mess behind, Kerry came out of her room. Mr. Reynolds opened the drapes in the living room, and Mrs. Reynolds sucked in her breath. "Oh, Harold, the view is gorgeous!"

Mr. Reynolds smiled. "Do you like it?" He looked at Kerry, his eyebrows raised. Kerry nodded, wondering why no warm shivers raced through her at the sight of something so beautiful. She didn't even care to stay and stare at it. All her life she had dreamed of living somewhere where she could see the mountains like that. But now, it didn't matter.

"I'm going to finish unpacking my room," she announced.

Mrs. Reynolds turned away from the view. "Tell you what. I really need your help. So why don't you come into the kitchen after you hang up your clothes."

Kerry nodded and started to walk away.

Mr. Reynolds caught her arm as she passed. "Kerry," he said, his voice soft and loving. "I think you'll like it here."

"I know, Dad. It's just that. . . ."

Mr. Reynolds hugged her. She laid her head on his chest and wished it were Jack.

Halfway to her room, she turned around. "Mom, when do we get the phone?"

Mrs. Reynolds looked at Mr. Reynolds, waiting for an answer. "I think tomorrow," he said.

"Oh. I'll be out in a few minutes, Mom."

Kerry hung up her clothes, noticing she had forgotten to return a sweater to Justine. She took it off the hanger and held it for a moment, trying to decide if she should send it back, or keep it. Having part of Justine with her would be so comforting.

***

The cold air is going to ruin my voice, Kerry thought as she walked to school. *I get hoarse when the air is this cold.* She looked at the gray sky that dulled the color of life around her. She was angry at everybody today. She was angry at her dad for moving her to this awful place. She was angry at her mom for making her go to her first day at school alone. *Mom is too scared to come, but she'll send me. Why doesn't she just take another pill so she can help me?*

The school was so familiar, and so unfamiliar. It had the same gray lockers as Central High, the same graffiti on some, the same color green on the walls with the same green linoleum. But the kids were different, the doors different, the desks the same, yet different.

She clutched her notebook to her chest as she approached a group of girls. "Could you please tell me where the office is?"

"No!" they all said together, and then giggled. Kerry was too scared to laugh with them. She had done the same things to new kids at her school, but now it didn't seem so funny.

She waited a moment to see if they had been joking, and would now tell her where to go. The tallest girl did tell her where to go.

Kerry decided to look for the office on her own. She found it, and discovered it much like the office in her school, full of busy, overripe secretaries. She had never been sure if they were superbusy or supersenile. No one made a move to help her. Students pushed in and out, shouting orders to the secretaries who gave them what they needed.

Waving her hand to get some attention, Kerry called, "Excuse me," her voice sounding very small and gravelly.

One of the secretaries waddled over to her. "Yes?" she said, sounding breathless.

"I'm new here."

"Oh."

"I guess I'm supposed to go to school here."

"Where're your papers?"

"Papers?"

"Transcripts. Forms filled out."

"I haven't filled out any forms. My dad said my old school was supposed to mail you whatever you needed."

"Well, we haven't gotten anything."

A tiny voice called from behind the large secretary. "What's the girl's name?"

The lady at the counter let out a noise of disgust. "What's your name?"

"Kerry Reynolds."

The tiny voice called again. "We've got them."

"Then you help her," the counter lady said. "I got work to do."

The tiny voice came from an equally tiny lady. "Honey, you need to have your mom or dad fill out these forms. Didn't they come with you this morning?"

The kindness in the lady's voice made Kerry want to cry in her lap. "No, ma'am."

"Well you can take them home and bring them back tomorrow."

"We're not supposed to do that," called the other secretary.

The tiny secretary's voice got very firm. "The girl's a senior. She's responsible."

"No high-school kid is responsible."

The tiny lady smiled warmly, pushing the papers across the counter. "You bring these back tomorrow morning, okay?"

"Okay."

The tiny lady looked around to see if anybody watched. She put her wrinkled hand on top of Kerry's, lowering her voice to a whisper. "And if you need any help, you just come talk to me, okay?"

Kerry tried to smile back. "Okay."

The lady went to a file cabinet, and returned with a computer printout. "Here's a list of your classes. I wish we had a map for you, but we don't. You'll just have to find the classes on your own. Of course all the classes beginning with a one are on the first floor, all the classes beginning with a two are on the second floor. This is building A, and the other is building B. Very simple. Okay?"

"Okay."

***

Justine sat in the grove, across the table from Jack. "Do you miss Kerry?"

"Stupid question."

"Just trying to make conversation."

"Listen to Larry, he's making enough conversation for the both of us."

Justine started to laugh. "His mouth does have a habit of running on, doesn't it?"

"He has a favorite theme song, you know."

"Oh, yeah, what's that?"

Jack got up from the table and started to do a little dance. He held a banana in his hand, and sang into it. "Let me, entertain you. . . ."

Laughter rippled through the grove, as Larry grabbed the banana from Jack. "And *now* ladies and gentleburgers. We have for you, yes, just for you, in this audience, a famous comedian!"

Everyone applauded. Larry held up his hand for quiet. "But you all must be very quiet, for he is frightened of crowds. Presenting. . ."

Everyone looked at Jack, who had his hand over his face. "... Larry Moser!"

Jack stood and applauded while the rest of the crowd booed and moaned. When he sat down, Justine was still laughing. "Oh," she said, "I wish Kerry could be here too. I miss her nose scrunching up and her eyes laughing at Larry."

"Me too," Jack said. "I'm going to miss her more on prom night. The prom committee just asked me to emcee."

"Terrific!"

"Yes and no. I love to emcee, but how can I go to the prom without Kerry?"

"Ohhh," Justine let out a small groan. "No fun in going to the prom alone, is there?"

Jack turned sideways to watch Larry, chuckling at his antics.

"Who would emcee if you didn't?" Justine asked.

"You're looking at him."

Justine rolled her eyes. "Not *Larry*."

"You bet."

"Then you've got to save the senior class!" she said in mock horror.

"That's right!" he said, pounding the table with his fist. "It's a risky job, but someone must do it. I'll be the white knight. I'll save the people of the kingdom, you watch and see!" Jack held his fist in the sky for victory, while Justine clapped.

Then his face grew serious. "I will do it. I guess I'll just go alone. There really isn't anybody I want to be with besides Kerry. You don't think her folks would let her come out for the prom do you?"

"I think they'd let her, I just don't think they have the money to send her."

"I thought this job was so much better, and paid more."

"That will be true in a while, I guess. At least that's what Kerry told me her dad said."

Jack watched Larry. Justine could tell Jack wasn't paying attention, but was thinking deeply. Then a light went on behind his eyes. "I've got it!"

Justine tilted her head, her eyebrows raised. "What?"

"Why don't you come to the prom with me?"

Justine was confused. "Me? But. . . ."

"No, listen. I love Kerry, right?"

"Yeah."

"But Kerry can't go with me. You are her best friend. You are my friend too. You don't have a date for the prom yet, right?"

"Right," Justine answered, still confused.

"Then we'll go as friends, so neither of us misses out on the prom. Kerry shouldn't be jealous, because she trusts you, and won't feel threatened by some other girl."

Justine shook her head. "I don't know, Jack. I'll have to ask Kerry."

"Let me talk to her first. It was my idea, and she'll probably let me have it if it's a stupid idea."

"I—I guess so. But I won't say yes for sure until after I talk to Kerry. I want to hear her reaction for myself. I don't want to destroy a friendship because of a dance."

Jack reached across the table and shook her hand once. "It's a deal then. I'll ask Kerry in a few days, after she's had a chance to get settled."

Justine counted on her fingers. "Just think, Jack. With the time difference, she's out of school already."

"Lucky dog."

***

Kerry chose her favorite book from the shelf above her desk, *Anne of Green Gables.* She opened it and began to read. The words were as flat as a Coke left overnight in the kitchen sink. She replaced it and reached for *Where the Red Fern Grows*. It was flat too. So were all her favorites—*Jacob Have I Loved, The Arm of the Starfish*. . . . Book after book, reached for, opened, discarded. The books were as interesting and useful as a pile of rocks. She picked up a piece of paper and a pen, writing each word with precision.

> The sky is blue, but I only see it as gray. Dull, ugly world. Of course there is so much I don't see. My room is my country, the apartment, my world. To venture out is to go into inner space. And I never wanted to go into space. I only wanted to be with my friends and to sing, and that's gone too.

Crawling under her bed, she felt safe. Something was slipping. What was it and where was it going? Kerry was so scared. She wished she could crawl deep in the earth, and sleep.

❦ **10** ❧

❦In each class, Kerry felt she might as well be a squished bug on the wall for all anyone cared. It was as if everyone made a point of ignoring her. She walked home alone, wishing she were back at Central. *Wishing isn't going to get me anywhere.* She lifted her chin and walked proudly.

At home, she went into her room to do her homework. *If I don't have any friends to distract me, maybe I'll get better grades.*

Twice she went into the living room to turn down the TV. Her mom sat glued to it, still in her robe, with her hair sticking out every which way. "Mom, why don't you get dressed?" she asked.

"Why? There's nothing to do."

Kerry sighed and retreated to her room. She found it hard to concentrate. Her head kept going blank.

At nine, the phone rang. Everyone jumped, after so many days of quiet without any calls. Mr. Reynolds smiled. "It's for you, Kerry."

Kerry took the phone from her dad. "Hello," she said cautiously.

"Hi, sweetie!"

"Oh, Jack, I'm so glad it's you." She picked up the phone and walked into the hall, the cord trailing behind.

"Who'd you expect, the Pillsbury Doughboy?"

The corners of Kerry's mouth tugged gently.

"Hey, you aren't laughing."

Kerry tried to put on her best voice. "I'm smiling, though!"

"I miss you."

"I miss you, Jack. How's everyone?"

"Everyone's fine except me and Justine. We miss you too much."

"Ahhh. That's nice."

"So how's your new school?"

"It's okay. It's school."

Kerry knew she should be so excited that Jack called, but she couldn't seem to get up the energy, or something. She felt funny inside. Like she wanted to laugh, cry, scream, or do nothing at all.

She watched the minutes tick by, knowing it wouldn't be long until he would be gone and she would be aware of how alone she was in the apartment.

"Kerry, I want to ask you something."

"Hey, this sounds serious," Kerry tried to tease.

"Well, it is and it isn't. The prom committee asked me to be the emcee, and I wanted to do that, but I didn't want to go to the prom without you."

Kerry swallowed hard. "Go ahead and invite someone else. It's okay with me."

"I don't want to go with anyone else. I want you to come with me."

"I can't, Jack. . . ."

"Are you sure your parents can't fly you out?"

Kerry thought about the bare cupboards and the near-empty refrigerator. "Quite sure."

"Well, what if Justine went as my friend? Just so I don't have to sit alone at a table and feel like the third wheel."

"Of course. What a great idea." Kerry forced her voice to go up higher to sound excited.

"You don't mind?"

"Of course not. I would hate for you to be bored at the prom, and I trust Justine with you totally."

"Only if you're sure, Kerry."

"I'm sure I love you, Jack."

"I love you, Kerry. You're the best thing that's ever happened to me. I gotta go. My dad's yelling at me to get off the phone."

Kerry hung up the phone, her mind confused. She could trust Jack. She could trust Justine. They would have a good time being friends, laughing, joking, maybe even dancing. *But not a slow dance. They wouldn't do that.*

But still, something didn't fit.

"It's time for bed, Kerry," her father called.

"Can I call Justine first, Dad?"

"Okay, but don't talk too long."

Justine's voice sounded right next door, and that hurt, because she wasn't. She, like Jack, didn't seem to be sad at all. She said she missed Kerry, and Kerry believed her. So why didn't they feel as sad as she did?

"So you're going to go to the prom with Jack?"

Justine thought the question sounded like an accusation. "Well, I hadn't said I would yet. I wanted to ask you first. I would never do anything to hurt you. So if you would be upset, then I won't go."

Kerry pressed her hand against her forehead, trying to push out the hurting blackness. "I won't be upset," she lied.

Justine paused. "I still don't know, Kerry. I don't know if I believe you."

"Trust me, trust me!" Kerry sang. She felt her face crack with the smile she forced onto it. But she thought if she could smile, her voice would pick it up. Oh, how could she be so jealous? *See, I am so stupid.*

"So your new school is okay, huh?"

"Sure. Everything is fine, fine, fine."

Mr. Reynolds' voice boomed from the other room. "Enough, Kerry!"

"I gotta go. It's past my bedtime."

"Already?"

"Already."

"I sent you a letter, Kerry. You ought to get it tomorrow."

"Thanks, Justine."

Kerry tossed and turned, then lay wide awake thinking about the phone calls. She kept kicking herself inside for not being happy about Jack and Justine going to the prom together.

Jack and Justine. It already sounds like the perfect couple.

Would you shut up? Nothing's going to happen, and you know it.

She stared for a long time at Justine's sweater hanging over her desk chair. Nothingness filled her mind, her body. Funny how bad nothingness felt. Ugly. Had anyone before felt such pain? And lived?

She rolled over and looked at the clock. One-thirty.

***

Justine knocked on Claudia's door, and let herself in. "Justine! How nice to see you!" She hugged Justine, then pulled back to look at her. "Where's the pizzazz? The exuberance you carry with you?"

"I don't know, Claudia. Maybe because I miss Kerry. It makes it hard to sing."

"How long has she been gone?"

"Three weeks."

"Okay. Three weeks is a long time to you. But it's not going to help you two if you don't practice your singing. You learn, she learns. When you sing together, it will flow better than before."

Justine nodded, and put her cassette in the recorder. As she began the scales, her voice cracked several times. Claudia stopped in the middle of the third set and looked at her sternly. "Justine. You did not warm up your voice. You must take care of your instrument, or you will ruin it. Do not come again without being warm. I will not teach a student who does not care about the instrument. Kerry or no Kerry, you warm up your voice."

She worked Justine extra hard. In the middle of the lesson, Justine found a new strength and resolve. Five minutes before the end of the lesson, Justine stopped Claudia.

"I know what to do, Claudia. I will work extra hard. Can you suggest some music to practice with?"

There was a knock at the door, and another student walked in. "Mark! How nice to see you!" Claudia sang, brushing past Justine to give him a hug. She turned to Justine. "Justine, this is Mark. Mark, Justine."

A tall, dark-haired wonder gave Justine a shy smile. His chocolate brown eyes swept to the ground. "I'm sorry to interrupt."

"No, no," Claudia said with a wave of her hand. "We were having a discussion about music, just waiting until you came." She hugged Justine and whispered in her ear, "Re-

member to warm up." Then aloud, "I'll have some sugges-
tions for you next week."

"Thanks," Justine said as she returned the hug. She gathered her music and tape. "Nice to meet you," she called to
Mark.

***

The bathroom smelled of sweat and dirty socks, as well
as a mixture of odors that belonged there. Four dirty white
tennis shoes poked their noses underneath the stall doors.
Kerry stood on one foot, and then the other. The two tennis
shoe owners chatted back and forth. Their voices lowered
as one inquired of the other.

"Have you noticed the new girl?"

"You mean blondie? Ain't she a bore?"

The first girl snickered. "Not only that. Have you seen
her during workout? She's such a klutz, she can't do a decent jumping jack."

"Yeah. Her thighs bounce more than what's inside her
bra."

"If anything *is* inside there."

"Have you seen the fool guys drooling over her?"

"No kidding. And why, I'll never know. I think this shy
act is all a put-on. She's probably just casing us to see
what's what. She'll be another Sarah Greengate, you mark
my words."

"You really think so? Hey, pass me some paper. Did you
hear she wants to be a *singer?*"

"Hah! That's the joke of the century. Someday—I'll
never get this zipper up—she'll see what a fool she is.
People like that shouldn't be allowed out of the house in
the morning."

The flushing toilets mingled with cackling laughter. As
the doors shoved open, Kerry hid behind the doorjamb.
Then she walked around, as if she were just coming in. The
two girls looked at each other, and burst into laughter.

Kerry went into a stall, shoved her fingers down her throat, and threw up her lunch.

***

Everywhere Kerry looked, kids laughed and had a good time. She walked with her head down, afraid the kids were laughing at her. She wondered how many of them felt like the girls in the bathroom—probably a lot, by the looks of things.

Everyone loved her English class. The teacher had most of the kids laughing almost every day. Everyone except Kerry. The laughter and the fun separated her from the rest. She couldn't laugh. Didn't they understand nothing was funny anymore?

***

That night, Justine called Kerry to report how her voice lesson went. Kerry's high, pinched voice sounded as though she was forcing happiness. "Justine! Pretty soon no more pudgy thighs!"

"What?"

"I've lost twenty pounds! Aren't you proud of me?"

"Kerry," Justine replied, shocked. "You were only fifteen pounds overweight."

"Well I'm on my way to the perfect weight now."

"On your way? Kerry, are you eating?"

"Sure I'm eating. I've just decided not to eat so much."

"So how's school?"

Kerry hesitated to answer. "It's fine. I even got asked to the prom by three different guys."

"Terrific! Are you going?"

"Of course not."

"Why not?"

"Because of Jack. Besides, the guys here like to tease me about my California accent. And they think all California girls are loose. They're mad at me because I won't go out with them. They call me stuck up."

"But Kerry, you don't have to worry about that. They'll know in five minutes what fools they were. I think you should go."

"I'm not."

Justine pulled on the phone cord, letting the coils surround her finger. Her voice grew soft. "Do you have any friends yet?"

"No," Kerry answered bluntly. "I don't seem to fit in."

"But Kerry, you fit in everywhere."

"Not here."

"Your smile, your laugh, everyone likes them."

"Oh."

When Justine hung up the phone, she felt as though she had been talking to a stranger. A stranger she didn't like at all.

❧ **11** ❧

❧ "Come in," Kerry called in response to the knock at her bedroom door. She stuffed the paper she wrote on under her mattress.

Mr. Reynolds opened the door, came in, and sat on the corner of the bed. "Do you realize it's midnight, Kerry?"

"Oh, really?" Kerry said, trying to sound surprised.

"Yes, really. It isn't good for you to continue to stay up this late every night."

"It's okay, Dad. I'm writing songs. You know how I get when I'm writing. If I don't get it down now, then I won't get it down at all."

"Where is it?"

"Where is what?"

"The song you're writing."

"Oh, Dad, you know you can't see it in the rough stages. I get too embarrassed. It's awful."

Mr. Reynolds looked around the bed. "I guess I just wondered where it was."

"Here's my pencil," Kerry said, holding it up.

Mr. Reynolds shook his head as he sat on the end of her bed. "How are your voice lessons going?"

"Okay, I guess. It sure isn't Claudia."

"Is that why you are slacking off?"

"What do you mean?"

"Mrs. Thornton called me today. She asked if there was a problem at home. She said you aren't warmed up when you come in, that you don't try, and you aren't taking care of your voice. That's not like you, Kerry."

"It's the cold air. It changes my voice."

Mr. Reynolds rubbed his stubbled chin. Then he sighed. "I'm going to bed. And you must do the same."

"Yes, Dad."

Kerry pulled the covers over her head and lay there thinking, although there was nothing to think about. Her mind dropped in pieces of information mixed with other pieces of information. The thoughts slipped in and out without her thinking much about them. It didn't really matter.

The next night, she called Justine after her parents went out. She had been forbidden to call, because during the first three weeks, she had racked up too much in phone bills.

"Justine," she whispered, "God is not here."

Justine did not like the pinched sound to Kerry's voice. The bubbly was all gone. The stoic "Everything will be okay" was gone.

"Oh, Kerry, yes He is. He promised to go with you," Justine encouraged.

"Well, He broke His promise then, Justine. He's not here."

"Just reach out in the dark for Him. He's with you, Kerry."

The silence choked Justine. She felt a shiver run down her spine. "Kerry? Are you there?"

A tiny, quiet voice answered. "I'm here. You tell God for me that I need Him, okay?"

"Okay," Justine whispered back.

"It's ugly, Justine. It's ugly, and I can't take it anymore."

"Colorado is ugly?"

Kerry sighed. "You don't understand either, do you?"

Justine felt panic. "I'm trying to, Kerry. But you need to be more clear. Help me understand."

"Sometimes I wish I could go to sleep and never wake up. I don't like it here. I've prayed that God will let me come back to California, but He doesn't listen. He says to ask and keep on asking, and He'll answer my prayer, but He doesn't. Where is He?" Kerry picked at her ear. She pinched it, then started scratching the lobe with her fingernail until it started to bleed.

"I don't have any answers, Kerry."

"I'm an awful person, Justine. You know that better than anybody. I'm grateful that you put up with me for so long."

"Kerry, I didn't *put up* with you. You're my friend."

"You and Jack have a great time at the prom next week, okay? And write to me, okay, Justine?"

"I love you, Kerry."

Kerry hung up the phone. She went to her room and pulled out some paper. She sat there and wrote nothing. She noticed Emma dancing on the shelf. "You shouldn't dance, Emma. Dancing is for happiness. There is no more happiness. If you can't stop dancing, I'm going to have to send you away." Kerry stood her on the end of the bed, and looked at her. Emma kept dancing.

Kerry walked into her parents' room and dug through their closet looking for a box and tissue paper. She wrapped up Emma in them, and then wrapped it all up in brown paper. "I'm going to send you where you'll be taken care of," she whispered.

***

Justine held onto the phone for a few brief moments after she heard the click. She hung up the phone. "I don't get it, God," she said.

She found her mother knitting in front of the TV. "Mom? I'm worried about Kerry."

"Why's that, honey?"

"She's saying weird things about God not being around, and how ugly it is in Colorado, and stuff like that."

Mrs. Crawford put down her knitting. "Honey, Kerry has had to make a big move at a bad time in her life. You would feel just as angry and upset if we took you out of this school during your senior year. She has some adjustments to make, some things to give up. It's not easy for her."

"I don't know, Mom. I don't like what she says."

"You've got to think too, Justine, that maybe Kerry is having her period. You know how depressed you get right before yours."

"But Kerry has never been upset about *anything*."

"Then this will be a new experience for her. You mustn't let her lean on you too much. That wouldn't be helpful for her. If she knows you're there, she might not find the new friends she needs."

***

Justine took her thoughts to Jack the next day. She didn't want to worry him, so she smiled, and asked innocently, "Jack, have you talked to Kerry lately?"

"Sure, last night."

Justine wondered at his happy tone of voice. "How was she?"

"Terrific. She was cheerful, happy, said how everything was fine. She's written several songs." Jack laughed. "She even said she is hiding them under her mattress because she is so excited about them, she's afraid someone will see them before they're finished."

"She didn't sound sad or anything?"

"Not at all. She said she's going to be sending you something special in a few days when she can get to the post office—probably on Saturday morning. She said she wouldn't need it anymore and that you might like it."

Justine felt that fear swell inside her. "Did she say what it was she was sending?"

"Nope. Just that she knew you'd like it."

Justine bit into a cookie. She sipped Coke from a paper cup.

"Is that a Cherry Coke?"

"Hmm?" Justine asked, popping out of her reverie.

"Is that Cherry Coke or the regular stuff?"

"Cherry. Want some?"

"Sure. Hey, have you chosen your dress for the prom yet?"

"Mom and I are going to get it this afternoon."

"Okay. I'm looking forward to this. I wish Kerry were going. Gosh, I miss her!"

***

Kerry took her mom's car keys from the hook. She checked her purse to make sure she had some money, grabbed a couple of tapes, and wrote a quick note to her parents. "I got lonely and hungry. Went to the mall."

She turned onto the freeway, and pressed the gas pedal into the floor. She stared ahead, winding through the slow-moving cars. Once, she looked down at the speedometer and noticed it read seventy-five. Her eyebrows went up in pleasant surprise. When she looked again, she was headed toward the center divider. She slowly moved the steering wheel in the opposite direction. She almost didn't want to change course. *Dad would be so mad if I cracked up the car.* She looked at the divider longingly.

The mall at home in California was a friend. She could sit for hours, or browse for hours. She knew the personality of each store. She ran into people she knew, and somehow, even the people she didn't know were familiar.

As she walked through the Mountview Mall, she felt more alone than ever. Each face was intent on the job to be done. Friendly faces were only friendly with the people they shopped with. She didn't see anyone she knew, and no one looked familiar. She felt like a three-year-old lost in a department store—where everyone else was bigger, and knew what they were doing. They all had a purpose in life. Kerry was there because she had no purpose.

Kerry bought an ice cream, took two bites, then threw it in the trash. She pulled on her stringy hair, and hiked up her falling pants. She thought that perhaps she ought to go home and wash her hair. *When was the last time I washed it? Yesterday? No. Sunday? Oh. It was a week ago. I guess it's time.*

Kerry drove home, arriving before her parents. She crumpled the note she had written, and climbed into bed. She lay there staring at the ceiling for minutes, for hours.

❧ **12** ❧

❧**K**erry walked back and forth across her room. She couldn't sit still, not for one more minute. She wanted to get out, out of this crazy house, out of her crazy life. She held an envelope in her hands, pulling out the letter to read again and again. "We're sorry . . . ," it said.

"Sure you're sorry. You're not sorry. You hated my tape. Let's face it. You hated me. You hated my voice. You hated my song. I'm no good, and I never will be."

Something wound up tight inside. Something all tied in knots, that wound itself up tight with the knots. It started somewhere. But where? Where do you start to untie a tiny necklace when it gets knotted up? Where do you begin to unravel a life that is all knotted up?

It's useless. As useless as untying that knotted chain. You throw it away. You toss it. Get rid of it. You get rid of useless toasters when they don't work anymore. You throw away things that don't work.

***

Justine put on her dress. She wished she could have gotten a Gunne Sax, but they looked silly on her. Instead, she chose a white Classic with full, puffy sleeves that reached down to her elbows. The fabric was plain, but the cut of the dress made it special. It was cut low in the back, with a scoop neck in front. She turned around in front of the mirror, thinking that maybe beauty was all in the clothes. She actually looked more than plain tonight!

She loved the way her mom's friend had done her hair. She had worked for two hours curling, pinning, and spraying. She French braided one strand, and wrapped it around to the other side. A loop of hair here, and another in the back. Straight down the center of her back hung the bulk of her black hair. She only hoped the curls would last the night.

She tucked a sprig of baby's breath into the front loop. Something didn't seem quite right. She went down the hall to the bathroom to get her makeup.

***

Kerry turned on her favorite tape, and her heart began to cry—while her eyes stayed dry. Thoughts rushed into her brain like floodwaters burying a Latin village. Everything inside is muddy. Everything inside is useless.

She tried to sing, but her voice came out scratchy, like an old record.

She felt so cold. She opened her closet to add a sweater to her blouse. Justine's sweater caught her eye. She put it on, expecting to feel Justine's warmth and friendship.

Justine was going out with Jack. To the prom. Tonight. She looked at her clock. It was five-twenty. Her parents said they'd be home by six-thirty, after an early dinner with Dad's new boss. Only one more hour, and she wouldn't be alone anymore.

She picked up the envelope and stared at it. "What a day for another rejection to come. Isn't anyone going to want my music?" She pulled the letter out and tacked it to her bulletin board. *Sixteen rejections. No one is going to want my music. Ever.*

***

Justine couldn't stop the excitement swelling inside her. The prom. She didn't want to sit down and wrinkle her dress. She didn't want to walk around in her heels, or her feet would hurt before the end of the night.

She wished she were going with a boy she liked, and one who liked her. She closed her eyes and pictured his arm around her waist, pulling her close. She would look into his eyes and smile, but not too big. Just enough to let him know. . . .

She shook her head. *Going to the prom with a friend is better than not going at all.*

In her mother's room, she turned slowly in front of the full-length mirror. *Nice. I hope Jack thinks so.* For a minute, Justine wished Jack liked her instead of Kerry. She stuck her tongue out at herself in the mirror. She would never do that to her best friend, *never!*

***

Kerry sat on the bed and moaned. She looked at her calendar. Long before she knew they would have to move, she had circled that night with a thick purple marker. The prom. Her senior prom. Since the sixth grade, she had been looking forward to the time when she would be a senior.

She would wear a beautiful pink dress, with a corsage of white roses.

And now her dream was shattered. And besides that, her boyfriend and best friend were going together. Kerry curled up in a ball on her bed, too weak to battle the monsters attacking her within. They reminded her that she was no good. She couldn't even get an *A* in music. She had no friends now. The kids at school called her the California Dreamer. "Hey, Dreamer!" the kids would shout as she walked down the hallway at school.

Something had poked a hole her life, and all that she was, simply flowed away. There was nothing of worth left.

Kerry wandered through the small apartment. She went into her mom's room and sat on the big bed. She thought of Goldilocks and the three bears. Goldilocks tried out everything and nothing was right. Kerry reached over to grab the phone. *I'll call Justine.* As she picked up the phone, she knocked over a bottle of pills.

She looked at them, her mind encouraging her.

***

When the doorbell rang, Justine grabbed her shawl. She hated it, but didn't have anything else to wrap around her dress. A coat or a sweater would look so awkward. Her mother suggested the shawl. It *was* pretty with a golden thread woven through it. But a *shawl?*

Jack stood inside the door, talking with her father. Justine sucked in her breath, wishing Kerry could see him. His tux was an antique brown, with a satin handkerchief poking out of the breast pocket. In his hand, he held a small box.

As he looked at her, she could see the admiration in his eyes. She loved it, but she felt, somehow, that it betrayed Kerry.

"Justine, you look nice," he said casually.

"Thanks, Jack, you do too."

Jack opened the box in his hand, oblivious to Justine's

parents snapping pictures every minute or so. He lifted out a small corsage with two yellow carnations. He handed it to her. "All the girls will have them," he said shyly. "I didn't want you to be left out."

Justine's heart melted. "Kerry always said you were considerate."

Jack looked down at the floor. "I hope you don't mind my saying this. . . ."

He stopped, as if afraid to finish the sentence. Justine looked at him. "Yes?"

Jack looked at her parents. "Later."

Justine nodded.

He hesitated a moment, then asked. "Justine, would you mind if we called Kerry? It might make her feel better. I sent her a great big bouquet of flowers, but they said I called too late and they couldn't deliver them until Monday."

Jack turned to Mr. Crawford. "If you don't mind our using your phone, sir. I've gotten permission to use my father's credit card."

"Fine with me, Jack," Mr. Crawford said.

Justine tried not to laugh at Jack's change in voice and manner. So formal and adult.

Jack punched in all the numbers on the phone. Justine went to the extension phone in her mother's room and listened to the ring.

***

It will be all over, it told her.

No more pain.

She took one pill, and then another, and another until she lost count. Once she began, it was easier to go on.

Her trembling hand picked up the phone and dialed Justine's number. She prayed Justine would be there and notice her sleepy voice.

"Hello, Joey? This is Kerry. Is Justine there?"

"Joey? I'm sorry, you must have the wrong number."

Kerry's mind was getting a little fuzzy. She dialed the number again, trying hard to remember each one, and to make sure her finger hit the right button.

"I'm sorry, you have the wrong number," another voice said.

Kerry hung up the phone, forgetting who she was trying to call in the first place. "I guess I'll go to bed now," she said to herself. She went back to her room, and put on her pajamas. She wasn't sure why she did it. She only knew that she was very tired, and not feeling real good. She felt horrible. And when you are sleepy and feel horrible, you go to bed.

As she climbed into bed, she noticed her clock said six-thirty. "Oh, good. They'll be home soon. That will be soon enough." Who was coming, and what they would be soon enough for, she wasn't sure. She just wished she felt better. She couldn't remember ever feeling so sick in her life.

One more hour, she thought. *They'll be sure to come home in one more hour. They'll take care of me. Maybe then we can move back to California.* Her eyes refused to stay open. It was getting hard to breathe. *And then I'll go to the prom with Jack, and Justine will help me write the song that's spinning in my head. Oh, head, please stop. It hurts. Oh God, it hurts.*

The phone rang and rang.

Kerry wondered what noise beat on the fringe of her brain. The phone! Her brain shrilled with each ring. The phone! *Why answer it?* Little tears dripped down the sides of her face. *It's not for me. No one loves me.*

Pretty soon she forgot about the phone, and snuggled down into bed.

***

Jack was disappointed when he hung up the phone. Justine could tell because the excited look was gone from his face. Not only that, he had let the phone ring thirty times, hoping Kerry would walk into the apartment and answer it.

I guess I don't have to worry about this being anything but a friendship date, Justine thought. *Now I can have a good time, and not worry about whether or not my actions will hurt Kerry. Jack is certain to be careful.*

Jack opened the car door for Justine. As he slid in his side, he gave her the schedule for the evening. "We'll go to the pre-prom party at Frank's house, then be at the Hyatt at eight. If, by the time the prom is over, we're still awake, your father said it was okay for us to go to breakfast at Okino's at the beach."

"Sounds great, Jack." Justine looked at her nails, inspecting them for any smudges in her polish. She was shy about saying her next thought. She had practiced saying it in front of the mirror, so her nervousness wouldn't make it sound fake.

"Jack, this is really sweet of you to take me. I know you'd rather be with Kerry, and all. And I wouldn't have been able to go to the prom . . . I . . . thanks."

Jack drove for a few more blocks, not responding until they stopped at a signal. "Larry would have asked you," he said softly, embarrassed.

Justine looked at him, startled. "Larry? How do you know? Why didn't he?"

"He heard I asked you. I, uh," Jack cleared his throat, his ears turning bright red. "I knew, but I really didn't want to go to the prom alone. I didn't know anyone else I could go with and not worry they'd take it wrong. . . ."

Jack looked at her, then quickly looked away. Justine started to laugh. "I hope you know, you saved me from a fate worse than death."

Jack threw back his head and laughed. "Well, now that's a relief."

❧ 13 ❧

❧*It's so strange to be in such an adult place, with only kids around.* Justine sat at the head table with Jack, Frank and Cathy, Larry and Eileen, and Pete and Kris. She could see out over the dance floor, with all the tables surrounding it. *It looks like a palace,* she thought, *with all the fine dresses, white tablecloths, and silver.* All the guys who looked so grungy at school were now gorgeous in their tuxes.

The dinner was mediocre, but Justine didn't care. She didn't come to eat, she came to enjoy herself.

After dinner, Jack stood to give awards, doing a three-minute routine at the beginning. Justine laughed so hard, her sides hurt. She hoped her mascara wasn't running down her cheeks with the tears. Larry guffawed in her ear.

As Jack announced the prom princesses and princes, he added little anecdotes about each. It was all ad-libbed, Justine knew, because he had no idea who had won the votes cast the week before by prom ticket holders.

Justine folded her napkin as Jack was about to announce the queen. She looked up after she heard the envelope open, because Jack made no sound. His face was one of shock, and his eyes had little tears in them. "The queen," his faltering voice announced, "is Kerry Reynolds." Justine was stunned. The room filled with applause, and many of the kids stood up.

Jack raised his hand for silence. "It says here that everyone wanted Kerry to know how much she is missed, and how much they appreciated her. So everyone got together and voted. It was unanimous except for two votes." He looked at Justine. "Yours and mine. They wanted to surprise us."

Justine smiled with tears in her eyes and looked down at her plate.

Larry jumped up from his seat, grabbing the microphone and remaining envelope from Jack's hand. He ripped open the envelope, and read. "The king is, of course, Jack Florez."

Jack looked even more stunned than before as the applause again filled the room. Larry spoke again. "Since the queen is absent, we will ask her best friend, Justine Crawford, to fill in for her."

Larry motioned Justine up to the front. Justine sat, frozen in her chair. The band began to play as Larry called out, "The first dance is for the king and queen and their court." The other couples eagerly got up to dance. Jack stepped down to the table and held out his hand. "C'mon, Justine. Kerry would want her substitute queen to fulfill her obligations."

Justine took his hand. She was embarrassed that all eyes

watched the few couples on the floor. Jack wasn't a great dancer. He was even more awkward than she. But pretty soon, his sly comments had her giggling, and feeling at ease again.

When they sat down, Justine leaned over to whisper to Jack. "Kerry will be so pleased that she was thought of that way. It was always her dream to be chosen prom queen. Mine too, but I knew I never had a chance."

Jack played with his dessert fork. Tears came again to his eyes. "I'm glad you both got your dreams ... but I wish Kerry could be here to enjoy it."

Justine watched the dancers on the floor. "Why does life have to twist sometimes? Where the person who deserves the best doesn't get it, and the one who doesn't deserve it, gets lucky?"

Jack touched her arm. "Life doles out good things to us sometimes, and sometimes it doesn't. Accept what's been given to you right now, because sometimes God seems to give happiness to help us through a sadness."

"You sound like my mother."

Jack chuckled. "Maybe she knows my mother. She's the one who told me all that."

"Do you believe it?"

"I don't know. It's hard to know what to believe sometimes. You're right. Life is all twisted and never seems to come out the way you think it should."

"But it does seem to come out right in the end, don't you think?"

Jack leaned back in his chair. He cast a sideways glance at her. "What end? When you're eighty-five?"

Justine shrugged. "I don't know what end. End of school, end of life? I don't know."

Larry leaned over them, holding on to Eileen's hand. "Would you guys quit the serious looks? You're supposed to be happy. Come on and dance."

Jack looked at Justine. "He's right for once. It's a fast one; we don't have to be on display this time."

"Okay."

***

"I am so sick," Mrs. Reynolds moaned. "I've never been this sick before. Stupid. I'm an idiot to eat shrimp."

Mr. Reynolds put his arm around her, gripping tight, keeping her from falling over. "The doctor warned you that your allergy to shrimp would make you very, very sick."

She struggled to put a finger to her lips. "Shh, shhh," she said, stumbling over an imaginary stair. "Kerry's sleeping. Oh! Maybe I'd better tell her we're home. I forgot to call her and tell her we were going to be home late."

"It's okay, Eloise. I'll check on her in a minute," he promised.

She nodded heavily. Looking startled, she asked, "Harold, why is the room spinning?"

"Eloise, lift your arms, that's it. We'll just get you in bed."

Eloise was asleep before her head reached the pillow. She hit her empty pill container with a stray hand, wondering what made the hollow noise.

Harold went to the bathroom and returned, never turning on the light. He crawled into bed and fell asleep, forgetting his promise.

***

Jack parked his car in Justine's driveway. He jumped out, opening Justine's door, before she had a chance. They walked to the front door in the silent night. "Jack, I don't think I've ever had more fun in my life," Justine whispered.

Jack smiled a sweet, sad smile. "I'm glad you had fun. I'm really grateful that you came. It would have been too bad to miss the prom because. . . ."

116

Justine put her key in the door. "See you on Monday."
Jack waited until Justine had closed the door, then strolled to his car. He looked up at the stars, and whispered. "Kerry, I miss you. I wish it could have been you tonight."

***

Mrs. Reynolds moaned. She rolled over and moaned again. Pressing her palms against the sides of her head, she muttered, "Harold, why does my head hurt so bad?"
Mr. Reynolds rolled over and put his arms around her. "It's from eating all that shrimp, then spending half the night in the bathroom."
"I don't like it."
"Then you shouldn't have eaten so much."
"Remind me never to do it again."
Mr. Reynolds chuckled. "I tried to warn you last night."
Mrs. Reynolds sighed. "I guess I just didn't care. Do you realize how depressing it is not to have any friends? I just wanted to laugh and have fun." Tears started to roll down her face. "I don't like it here, Harold. I want to go home."
"You'll get used to it, Eloise. It takes time to make new friends."
Mrs. Reynolds started to shake with quiet laughter. "You sound like me, when I tell Kerry the same thing." She faced him. "Do you think we did the right thing by moving here during her senior year?"
Mr. Reynolds kissed her forehead. "We can't look back now. What's done is done."
"I know, but. . . ."
"Shhh," he put his finger to her lips. "I don't want to hear anything more about it."
"But she's not sleeping well. . . ."
"She's sleeping this morning. Listen."
They both listened to the silence. Mrs. Reynolds' eyes grew wide. "Do you think she's okay?"

"Of course she's okay."

"But she's been waking up at four every morning."

Mr. Reynolds chuckled, pushing a stray hair from her face. "You mothers always find something to worry about. When she's up at four, you worry. When she's asleep at nine, you worry." He threw the covers off, and climbed out of bed. "What do you say we go to the late church service?"

"Do you think I should?"

"Don't be foolish, Eloise. I'll get in the shower; you go wake up Sleeping Beauty."

Mrs. Reynolds struggled out of bed and into her robe. She yawned and stretched as she stepped into the hall. In the next moment, she forgot her headache. Her life turned upside down, and would never be righted again.

***

Justine's mother listened in stunned silence as Mrs. Reynolds sobbed her way through a list of what-ifs.

"I should never have eaten that shrimp. We should never have stayed out without calling her, but I thought she was old enough, and it didn't matter. I should never have left those pills lying around, and we should have checked on her when we got home, but I was too sick to even stand up, and I guess Harold forgot, and my God, what are we going to do? . . ."

Mrs. Crawford couldn't give any comfort. There was none to give. After hanging up the phone, she went into the kitchen and poured herself a cup of coffee. She sat at the round oak table, resting her slippered feet on the claw feet of the table. She sipped the coffee, wondering how she would tell Justine.

She dropped her head on the table and prayed. She felt a little tap on her shoulder. Joey scrunched up his face in concern. "Are you sick, Mommy?" he asked.

Mrs. Crawford tried to smile, but didn't succeed. "No, honey, I'm not sick. But I am sad."

"Then why aren't you crying?"

Mrs. Crawford sighed. "Sometimes it hurts too much to cry, Joey."

"Oh. Can I have a cookie?"

"Yes, Joey. Then can you go see if Sammy can play with you this morning?"

Joey's face lit up. "Sure. Can I eat lunch there, too?"

"If his mommy says it's okay."

Joey skipped out of the house shouting, "Yippee, no church today!"

Justine padded into the kitchen just after Mrs. Crawford poured her third cup of coffee. She slid into a chair across from her mother, cupping her chin her hands. "Oh, Mom, I had the most *wonderful* time. Jack is a gentleman, and so totally stuck on Kerry that I never had to worry. And you'll never guess what happened."

"What?" Mrs. Crawford tried to answer calmly.

"All the kids elected Kerry prom queen! They wanted to let her know how much she is missed. When they took a picture of the court, they left the queen's throne empty. They're going to blow it up and send it to her. Wasn't that sweet?"

Tears started to well up in Mrs. Crawford's eyes. She nodded, but kept her eyes focused on the coffee mug in front of her.

"And since she wasn't there, they asked me to take her place as kind of a replacement queen. It was the best time I've ever had in my life." Justine closed her eyes and smiled, remembering.

Mrs. Crawford didn't feel it was right to tell Justine now, and ruin her memories of the prom. Nor did she feel it would be right to wait. She took a large gulp of coffee, then put her mug firmly on the table. "Justine, come over here," she said softly, patting the chair next to her.

Justine did as her mother told her, watching her mother, and suddenly noticing that things were not right. She began to shiver a little, wondering what her mother had to say.

Mrs. Crawford pushed her mug to the center of the table, and turned to face Justine. She put her hands on Justine's arm, then looked at her eyes. "Justine, I have some really terrible news."

Justine pulled back, her eyes widening.

"Kerry's dead."

Justine stared at her mother. She shook her head slightly, not wanting to hear. In a small whisper she said, "She's not."

Mrs. Crawford tightened her grip on Justine's arm. "She killed herself."

"No, Mom. Kerry wouldn't do that."

"She swallowed her mother's pills."

Stiff, straight, her eyes staring in front of her, Justine protested. "No, Mom, she didn't. She wouldn't. We love her. She's prom queen. She's alive, more alive than anyone I know." Justine bit her finger and looked at the yellow curtains, bright and cheerful in the sun.

"Mrs. Reynolds said she'd call Jack." Mrs. Crawford gripped her coffee mug and stared at Justine, wondering at her composure. Then, it shattered.

Justine yanked her arm away from her mother's touch and ran outside. She ran down the street in her robe, then up the hill. She ran to the porch of the pink stucco house, and hid in the corner. She put her head on her knees, then lifted her face to the sky and screamed.

❧ 14 ❧

❧ **W**alking to school, Justine didn't see any of the houses, any of the trees, any of the cars. She didn't even see the kids who swarmed around her, or the graffiti on the school sign.

Why am I here? Why did I come?

Maybe if I keep doing what I've always done, I'll find out it's not true. This is only a dream anyway. A terrifying, ugly dream.

She went through each class, sitting, opening her books, turning in her homework, closing her books, standing up, walking to the next class. Every movement was mechanical and computerized. She didn't want to see anyone. She didn't want to hear anyone. She wanted to scream again, but no scream came. No words came. No words, no feelings.

It's my fault. It's Jack's fault. We killed her. We just had to be selfish and go to the prom together. We killed her.

Lunch seemed somehow chaotic. Justine walked in fear among the kids, afraid that somehow, her life would spin out of control. It was too noisy, too uncontrolled. She wandered into the grove, and looked around.

Cathy let go of Frank, and walked solemnly to Justine. She wrapped her arms around her, and for a brief moment, put her forehead on Justine's shoulder. "Oh, Jussie," she whispered. "I'm so sorry."

Justine nodded, her limp arms hanging at her sides.

One by one her friends filed by. Some gave her a hug, some touched her shoulder. Pete and Larry both kissed her on the cheek. Larry gave her an extra squeeze to go along with it.

Justine stood for a moment, and looked around at her circle of friends. "Thanks," she said quietly.

Then, a flash of fear sent her running. Cathy's voice followed after her. "Don't, Larry. Let her go."

Yeah, Justine thought. *Let me go.*

She ran to the cafeteria, and sat in the nerds' corner. They left her alone, their noses firmly planted in their books.

Justine faced the wall, staring at the bumps on it, as she nibbled at her food.

A small voice came from behind her, startling her into remembering something she wanted to forget. "Justine, what am I going to do?" The chair next to her was pulled out, and sat in.

Justine reached over and patted Jack on the shoulder. He put his head in his hands and began to cry. Justine knew her gentle pat lacked the compassion Jack needed. She didn't have anything to give him.

His sobs subsided, and Justine picked at her food. Jack looked at her with reddened eyes. Justine clapped her hand over her mouth to stop a sudden laugh. Red eyes, red nose, red cheeks—it struck her funny, and she choked.

"Justine. I loved her. Why did she do it? She had so much to live for."

"Obviously she didn't," came Justine's cold answer. She stuffed her food in her sack, rolled it all into a little ball. She picked up her sweater, books, and bag. Walking away from a startled Jack, she threw her sack in the trash barrel and ran out of the room.

A plastic cup lay in the middle of a puddle of water. A gum wrapper floated by in the gutter. The birds took off in a black cloud of rushing wings. Justine stepped around a soggy newspaper, split apart by the wind, then soaked by the night rain.

Justine sighed, and tried not to cry. It almost sounded like hiccups had stuck in her throat. Spring. Spring was supposed to be the start of life, not the end of it. Friends weren't supposed to die. There was too much of life ahead, to be shared, to be enjoyed, to cry over. There was too much of life to scream at, to shake your fist at God for, and then to turn around and hug Him tight because *sometimes* the bad turned out okay after all.

But not this time. There would be no okay this time.

Justine wanted to scream at the people driving by, laughing. She wanted to scream at the birds singing in the trees, the flowers starting to bloom. She felt like the soaked newspaper, falling apart because of the events spiraling out of her control.

Ever since Kerry had moved, not a day went by that Justine hadn't wanted to talk to her, sing with her. Now Kerry had decided they would never enjoy each other again.

"Never?" Justine looked up at the breaking clouds. "Never, God?"

She thought she heard God cry.

***

On Tuesday, Justine used every ounce of energy to drag herself out of bed. Something seemed to weigh down every part of her body. She didn't want to go anywhere. Her mom offered to drive her to school, and Justine accepted. Neither said a word in the car.

She walked up the school steps, her head down. Scores of feet passed her. Conversation stopped around her. As she walked down the ugly green hall, she heard ugly whispers about ugly things. "Kerry," she heard, over and over, and it shook in her head.

She was glad for each class. Her mom said she didn't have to go to school if she didn't want to, but for Justine, it meant some sort of order in the chaos of her mind. If she sat at home, she would suffocate from all the thoughts. And she just might decide to join Kerry.

She couldn't face what Kerry had done, but she could pretend that it didn't happen. She could make sure the world was operating under some sort of order—even if it made her furious that it did.

Order, order, order. Control. Don't lose them. They're important.
Why?
I don't know.

The questions never left her alone. They pestered her during class, they interrupted dinner, they prodded her when she was alone in bed at night. *Why, Kerry? Why did you do it?*

How do you expect me to go on living when you have now said life isn't worth living?

Justine flopped back and forth in bed, trying to escape the questions. Each time she turned away from one question, another came. *Life is so ugly. It's so unfair.* Her dreams screamed questions in her head. Sleep came without rest.

***

Justine woke, wondering. "It's all been a bad dream, hasn't it?" she said to herself, hoping. As she swung her legs over the side of her bed, she saw the bruises on her thighs where she had kept pinching herself the day before to see if she was in reality, or dreaming this nightmare.

Her heavy, erratic breathing choked her. She wanted to escape. Escape from reality. Escape from ugly. Escape from the awful pain.

That's what Kerry did. She escaped from the awful pain. The awful reality of an ugly life.

"Justine," Mrs. Crawford sat on the bed next to her daughter, putting her arm around the stiff shoulder. "It's after nine, honey."

Justine stared at the clock. She had gotten up sometime before eight. Where had the time gone?

"You will want to go to the funeral, and so you'd better get ready."

Justine felt a terrible anger rumble inside her. "Yeah. Her parents can afford to fly out here for a funeral, but they couldn't afford to fly Kerry out for her prom."

"I guess they didn't know how important the prom was, or how much loneliness Kerry felt." Mrs. Crawford hated her feeble words.

"They didn't care about her." Justine turned on her mother. "And you didn't either. I told you how upset she was. How she wasn't eating, and scared, and lonely. You told me it was just a phase."

Mrs. Crawford hung her head, taking her arm from Justine's shoulder, wiping the tears from her eyes. "I . . . I hoped it was. I never thought happy Kerry would ever. . . ."

Justine lost her anger, slipping back to feeling numb. She stared at the wall, not noticing that her mother left. Sometime later, she went to her closet, and pulled out the first dress she touched.

She sat on her bed and waited.

***

The funeral home was stuffy. People fanned themselves with bits of paper, while overhead, ceiling fans chopped the muggy air. Justine sat in the second row, a seat away from the Reynolds. She stared at the flower-adorned casket. She stared, and stared, and stared. She wanted to see inside, and she didn't. She wanted to know Kerry was really dead, and she didn't.

Once, she looked at the Reynolds. She wanted to shout at them for ignoring Kerry, but she couldn't. She knew it was her fault, not theirs. She looked at them and thought how strange they looked. How pale, drawn, and closed up. Like the casket.

The pastor of her church stood at the pulpit. Justine felt angry again. Angry that a pat-answer man would stand up there and tell them things that didn't matter. Things that didn't make a difference.

The minister stood in a flowing black robe, his hands folded on the pulpit. Beads of sweat stood out in the bald streak through the center of his head. "Friends and loved ones of Kerry . . . ," he began.

Justine looked around, wondering when Kerry would pop out of the crowd, her hand covering her giggling face. She'd stop this whole crazy business with a smile.

She turned to the preacher, hoping he would reveal the hoax and call Kerry out from the back room. But he didn't. Nobody stopped the funeral. Everyone cried. Justine thought she even saw tears in the preacher's eyes, but she wasn't sure.

"Life is difficult and unfair," the preacher said. "Sometimes it is so unfair, that people choose not to go on. And we have here, one very precious one, who saw the unfairness and was overwhelmed by it.

"As I have spoken with her parents, we have agonized over *why*. They have shared with me that she was never one to see life as negative. She only allowed herself to see the positive. When they moved, she had no friends, was ridiculed for who she was, and for what she wanted to be.

"The day of her death, she received another rejection of her music. The label she most dreamed of sent her a letter saying they could not use her music.

"She would not go to the prom. She would not graduate with her friends. Her beautiful voice cracked when she tried to sing, because of the cold and because she no longer practiced.

"I want to read to you some things Kerry wrote in recent days, words on paper stuffed under her mattress."

I'm lonely, God, do You hear me? I hurt so bad. Somehow I've fallen into a dark, cold, lonely place. It's crushing me. Is this what hell is like? It must be. There is no pain as bad as this. Will somebody please love me? Will somebody please take away my hurt?

Justine felt herself stiffen in the chair, her mind calling out to Kerry. *Kerry, I love you. I'll take away your hurt. Just talk to me. I'm here, Kerry, I'm here.*

Why am I so screwed up? Why can't I be normal? Why is there no one out there to help me? How did I ever get like this? God, do *You* hear me? I want to get well. I don't want to die, but I'm dead inside. And there's no hope. Things aren't getting better. Somebody please hear me. Please help me.

Justine's ears opened to the sniffles and sobs across the room. She looked down the row at Jack. He sat stiff and tall in his suit. His eyes were dry, his hands fumbled and fidgeted.

Any decision I make will hurt me. I'm tired of fighting, tired of trying. Will I ever stop crying and start laughing again? What's the point? Who cares?

The minister paused and wiped his eyes with a handkerchief. His tearful voice came out as a loud whisper. "We care, Kerry, we care."

His hands squeezed the podium sides, and his thunderous voice made everyone jump. "We are all responsible for this child's death. Every single one of us. For we did not respond to her cries for help. When I leave here, I'm going to learn to hear those cries, so this does not happen to one of my 'children' again."

His fist thumped the podium, and he marched off the platform.

No one moved. The stunned organist had never had this happen to her before. She hesitated a few more moments, then started the machine wheezing out tunes. The people began to file by the closed casket, led by the ushers. Justine stared at the people as they touched the casket, and watched as some moved their lips silently.

Claudia walked by, her head bowed, the music gone from her movements. Larry, his shoulders bent as if he carried a heavy burden, scuffled by, his face wet with tears. Cathy cried so hard, Frank had to hold her up. He looked like he needed someone to help him.

Friend after friend, teachers, acquaintances, and people Justine had never seen before filed past, no one smiling.

When the building had emptied, except for the row that hurt the most, the usher came to them, and indicated they should also file by.

Justine stood next to Jack, and leaned into him for support. He put his arm around her, and she put her head against his chest. It didn't matter what Kerry thought anymore.

She touched the casket, and then began to stroke it, as though it were her friend's hand. The tears poured out from some hidden well. Jack leaned over and touched the casket. "Oh, Kerry," he mumbled. "Why did you do it? I can't go on living without you here."

Justine's tears stopped suddenly, and she kicked the cloth-draped gurney.

***

The casket was lowered into the ground. Justine felt the most important part of her insides ripped away, and dropped into the hole.

❧ 15 ❧

Justine sat on the couch, holding the package in her trembling hands. The handwriting and return address screamed Kerry. It was too spooky, too strange, to hold something that came from a person now dead. She turned it over and over in her hands. Joey jumped up and down. "Open it, Justine," he begged. "This is like Christmas, or a birthday, or something."

Mrs. Crawford pulled him aside. "Joey. I've got something special for you to do in the kichen." She winked at Justine, and led Joey away.

Justine ripped the brown paper slowly from the package. Lifting the lid to the box, she found a note, written in a shaky hand, unlike Kerry's. "Justine," it read. "I know you'll take good care of her, since I can't anymore. Kerry."

Shivers went up Justine's spine. Lifting off the mounds of tissue paper, she came face to face with a tiny Kerry—Emma.

"Oh, Mom," she called out.

Frightened by Justine's voice, her mother came running. Justine held up her arms, feeling like a baby, desperate to be one.

Mrs. Crawford saw Emma lying in the folds of tissue, and understood. She put her arms around Justine, and let her cry.

"Mama, I want Kerry to come back."

"Honey, there's no turning back death."

"But I want her to see how much we miss her, how much we love her."

"She never will." Mrs. Crawford pushed the mute button on the TV remote control. She pushed off her slippers with a toe. "I'm mad at Kerry, Justine."

Justine sucked in her breath.

"She snatched her life away from God. She had no right to end something God gave her."

Justine leaned toward her mother. "But Mom, she hurt so bad. Everything was going wrong. Everything that happened stabbed her, and took away her happiness. God wasn't there for her. If He cared so much, He could have stopped her. He didn't even try."

Mrs. Crawford shook her head. "You don't know that He didn't try. I'm sure He did. But God gave us a free will. That means we make our own choices—good or bad—God doesn't stop us, even though He gives us a chance. Besides, when things go wrong, even terribly wrong, does that give us the right to end our life? No, Justine. I'm sorry. She had lots of other options." Mrs. Crawford wiped angry tears from her eyes.

"Justine, I loved Kerry too. But what she did was selfish, ugly, and rotten."

Justine couldn't respond. She couldn't remember a time

when her mother had poured out her feelings like this. She poured out her love, many times, but never these kinds of feelings. It scared her.

Tears rolled down Mrs. Crawford's face, and splattered on her clenched hands. "She could have lived here, Justine. She could have gone to the prom. I loved her almost as much as I love you. Why did she do this? Why? She had so much to live for, she only had to wait it out."

Justine's feelings rumbled around inside her. She couldn't hold on to them long enough to figure out what they were. Her stomach churned, and her body felt quivery. "Mom," she said, her voice very small. "I don't like what Kerry's done to us." As soon as she said the words, she clapped her hand over her mouth.

Her mother nodded. "See, Justine. You feel it too. You just won't admit what a terrible thing Kerry's done. To herself, and to us most of all. She created a tragedy from which no one will recover totally. How can we?"

"But Mom, if what she did was so terrible, what if I do it too? What if I'm next? I think about it all the time. I wonder what it felt like for her. I wonder what it would be like to. . . ." Justine shuddered, frightened by the thoughts that pestered her, and encouraged her to do violent things to herself.

Mrs. Crawford wrapped her arms around Justine. "It's not going to happen to you. I'm calling a friend of mine, Dr. Wilson. We can go talk to him. Maybe we can straighten all this out."

"Mom? Will you go with me?"

Mrs. Crawford squeezed Justine tighter. "I will. I need to talk to him too. Why would such a precious child end the joy she brought to us all? Why?"

***

Jack walked down the mall concourse. His funeral tie hung loosely around his neck, the knot pulled down to his second shirt button. His eyes searched the crowds, looking, looking.

He didn't remember much of the funeral. He remembered the fringe on the edge of the altar cloth. Gold, but dirty. He remembered wondering if the funeral home ever washed it. He must have stared at that the whole time. He didn't even know what color the casket was, or what kind of flowers adorned it. Were there any flowers?

The night before, his heart had beat wildly. He wondered if he would live through the night. Or if he would take a length of his rope. . . . The fear overtook him that he might be next.

Suddenly, next to the music store, he saw a flash of blond hair. A toss of a head, the unmistakable movements of happiness and joy he had come to love. *"Kerry!"* he shouted. He began to run, the jacket he held over his shoulder flying behind him like Superman's cape.

Frantic, he searched for her again, but had lost her somewhere in a crowd. He ducked into the music store. No Kerry.

He ran back out into the mall. Gone. Jack dropped onto the nearest bench and began to sob.

***

The movement of life goes on around me, oblivious to my pain.

Justine never ceased to be amazed at the insensitivity of people around her. Didn't they know? Didn't they know the earth was no longer complete? Didn't they know and care and cry?

And what about God?

"God," she hissed. "You certainly have disappeared from the scene. Remember that day I became Your child? I gave my life to You. And You promised that when I did, You would never leave me. Did You forget already?"

Each step she took along the street, she stood straighter, and taller. Her breathing grew deeper and came faster. She glared at each person, daring them to be happy. Daring them to go on with life as if nothing had happened.

She walked faster and faster, then she started to run. The tears that had been locked up inside for two weeks began to gush in torrents. She ran past her house, up the street to the college. She hid in the forest of eucalyptus trees and brush across the street from Kerry's old house. She sat in their old hideout, and stared at Kerry's house.

"Kerry, I hate you. I *hate* you! Didn't you realize what you did to all of us? I used to feel sorry for you, but I don't now. I feel sorry for Jack. Do you know he can't even smile or tell a joke? He drags around and tries to do his work. But he can't even think. Why? Because of you.

"And your parents. I haven't seen them in a week, but the last time I saw them, they kept looking at each other and blaming each other. They would ask why, when they weren't blaming each other. They loved you, you little creep."

Justine wiped her face with her sleeve. She rubbed her running nose on her jeans. Her voice swelled with her anger, husky with tears.

"And what about me? You took all my dreams with you. You had no right to do that.

"You made me laugh. You made me think. You were my friend. It's not fair that you should die."

Justine picked up a rock and threw it through the bushes and into the street. She stood up, and went looking for a larger rock. She found several and heaved them through the bushes, hoping that they would crack the sidewalk, or hit a car. She wanted to hurt something. Most of all, she wanted to hurt Kerry, for hurting her.

***

Both Justine and Mrs. Crawford walked down the sidewalk without speaking. Hurried shoppers and business people brushed past them. Justine looked up at the door as her mother turned the brass knob. DR. MAYNARD WILSON, PSYCHOLOGIST. They walked through the empty waiting room, ushered immediately into Dr. Wilson's office. A comfortable couch sat against one wall of the room, an easy chair on either side of it. Dr. Wilson's desk was across the room. The book-lined walls gave the impression that they were in a library of an exquisite home, instead of in an office building in the heart of the shopping district.

Dr. Wilson warmly shook Mrs. Crawford's hand. "Please sit where you will be most comfortable," he encouraged.

Both Justine and Mrs. Crawford chose the couch, sitting at opposite ends.

"You ladies have taken the first important step in healing. You have agreed to talk about what's troubling you. Without that, you lock the pain up inside, and lock yourself away from anyone who can help you, or separate yourself from those who love you."

"Like Kerry did?" Justine asked.

Dr. Wilson smiled a gentle smile. "Like Kerry did." Dr. Wilson put his ankle across his knee. "You see, Justine, locking away such painful thoughts and memories does not make them go away. They will come back sometime, bigger and uglier than before, threatening to destroy you too."

Justine hung her head. "This morning I threw rocks in the street, hoping I'd hit a car by 'mistake.'"

"That's okay, Justine. You are angry at Kerry. That's a part of the healing process. You go ahead and be angry at her."

"But won't that mean I don't love her? I mean, I felt so guilty that I was mad. How can you be mad at a dead person? You're supposed to cry and be sad."

"You would be angry if someone stole a precious possession of yours. Well, Kerry stole something precious from you. She stole her life, her presence."

Mrs. Crawford reached over and touched her daughter's

arm. "I was angry at you, for having Kerry as a friend. For bringing this trauma into our family."

Justine looked shocked. She looked at her mother, then at the doctor. She spit words at him. "How can my mother be angry at me? It's not my fault."

"No, it's not your fault. Mrs. Crawford?"

"Justine, I had to be angry at somebody. Like you, I decided the anger I had for Kerry wasn't right. It had to go somewhere, and it landed on you. I'm sorry."

They talked for over an hour; questions, anger, guilt, and incredible pain poured into the room. Then, as if the flood had temporarily subsided, there was silence.

The doctor looked at his watch. "Our time is up, another patient is due to arrive. But I want to leave you with this, until next week. You will feel many emotions. You will feel terrible guilt. You will ask why until you would like to scream. You will cry, be angry, and hurt beyond belief.

"These emotions and more are a part of death, and magnified when the death is a suicide. Feel them, let them flow through you. If you try to ignore them, as I said before, they will come back to haunt you, twisting and distorting your life, your future. Take care of yourself. Do nice things for yourself and each other. And cry with each other. Ask the whys, and pretty soon, you will know that no true answer will ever come.

"One day you will find that in all this ugliness, her death will have made a profound change in your life. Part of it will always hurt. But another will drive you to be and accomplish something you never dreamed.

"Above all, pray. Talk to God about every single emotion and thought that passes through. Yell at Him. He can take it. He is as heartbroken as you about this."

They all stood; the close spell they had woven was now broken. Dr. Wilson shook their hands, then hugged them. "See you next week."

❧ 16 ❧

❧Justine sat in the car a moment longer. "Are you going to wait for me out here, Mom?"

"Yes. I brought a book to read. I'll come in if you want."

"I don't think so." She opened the door, and stepped out. "I'd better do it on my own."

Justine closed the door and went into the studio. Claudia swept over to her, more slow and subdued than before. "Justine," she said softly. "How nice to see you." She hugged Justine longer and tighter than usual. "I hoped you would come back."

"I almost didn't. I guess I feel dead."

Claudia put her arm around her shoulder. "The death of a friend kills a lot of things—your heart, your energy. You, especially, are accustomed to being carried by Kerry's dream. Pretty soon now, you will have to make a decision. Are you here for your dream? Or Kerry's?" Claudia's brow remained lifted for a few seconds, then she swept over to the piano, sat down, and began playing the scales.

Suddenly, Claudia sucked in her breath, and let out a sob. She began to play again, her chin up in the air, her face turned away from Justine.

Justine sang the scales, her voice a little hesitant. As she got into the routine, her voice became stronger, and she pushed aside the loneliness and aching pain of her heart. Five minutes before the end of her lesson, she brought out a song she had been working on since Kerry had died. She put it in front of Claudia, and stood back, proudly waiting for the praise.

Claudia hummed as she picked out the notes on the piano. Her head bounced with the rhythm. When she reached the end, she put both hands in her lap, and turned to look at Justine.

"It needs work. A lot of work."

Justine bowed her head, embarrassed.

"Look at me," Claudia ordered.

Justine looked up, little tears in her eyes.

"It is good. But it is bad also."

"Why is it good, and why is it bad?" Justine asked, her spirit backed against the wall, braced for the pain.

"It is good, because it has real feeling in it. It is musically good. But it is aesthetically bad."

"What does that mean?"

"It is too sad, too depressing."

"But it was meant to be sad."

"Songs should sometimes be sad, but never depressing. They should always celebrate life and creation."

"I still don't think I understand," Justine said, sitting on the stool.

"A song can speak of the sadness of life, but must somehow also celebrate it. If the words are very sad, there must be music that picks it up. If the music itself is quiet and slow, the words must do the celebrating. You see, even in sadness, there is something to celebrate."

"I guess I understand. Even though Kerry is gone, and I miss her friendship, I suppose someday I will find things to laugh about, beautiful things to look at, to fill the emptiness her being gone has made." She sighed. "At least that's what I'm told."

"You will never *fill* the emptiness," Claudia corrected. "The emptiness cannot be filled. It can only be decorated. So when you see the emptiness, it is not quite so ugly."

***

When Justine got back in the car, she looked at her mom carefully. She paused a moment, then asked, "Mom? What if I decide to stop singing?"

Her mom put a card in her book to mark her place and shut it. She placed the book on the seat next to her, then took Justine's hand. "You can do whatever you choose. Just don't make a decision until after graduation. You need some time to think things through. When something bad has happened is not the best time to make a big decision."

Justine smiled a crooked half smile. "You sound like Dr. Wilson."

Mrs. Crawford tilted her head. "That's because I heard it from him."

***

To Justine, it seemed to be night all the time now. She tried hard to see something fun in life, something worthwhile. But she only came up empty.

She stared at her books for hours on end. The only comfort she found, if it could even be called comfort, was in her singing. All too often, it only released the dam of tears, and she had to stop.

On Friday evening, the phone rang. When her mom handed the receiver to her, whispering that it was Mrs. Reynolds, something fluttered to life—an insane kind of hope. It told her that somehow, maybe a mistake had been made about Kerry.

"Justine? I want to read something to you." Mrs. Reynolds' voice sounded so strange. Quivery and unsure.

"Okay, Mrs. Reynolds."

"It's a letter from CBS Records."

Justine hesitated. "I don't know if I want to hear another rejection."

"No. You've got to listen," Mrs. Reynolds demanded.

"Dear Ms. Reynolds and Ms. Crawford:
    We showed your song 'Oh for the Joy' to producer Dan Jackson, who represents Shelly Grammercy. She would like to cut this song on her next album, which will go into production in two months. If you are still interested, please call us at (213) 555-6583 and we can start contract negotiations immediately. Ms. Grammercy would also like to see any other songs you have written."

Justine sat in stunned silence.

Mrs. Reynolds sobbed, "What are we going to do, Justine? Her dream came true too late. What are we going to do?"

"I don't know. I guess we should sign a contract. Then Kerry won't be completely dead," Justine said calmly.

"I'll send it to you, Justine. You do with it what you want. I don't want to hear about it. I'll send you any legal documents you need so it can all belong to you."

Numbed, Justine didn't know what to say. She listened to Mrs. Reynolds cry for the longest time. Then, without a good-bye, the phone was hung up.

Justine went back to her room. She sat on the bed. "Oh, Kerry. Why couldn't you have waited? Do you realize how lucky we are to be so young and to have a dream come true? So many people have had to wait years, and sometimes never see it happen. Why didn't you wait?"

A low, tired feeling swept over her. She crawled into bed, refused dinner, and went to sleep.

She stayed in bed all weekend, sleeping and thinking. Her thoughts didn't make much sense, and she couldn't remember what she had thought the moment before. She thought if she could stay in bed forever, she could forget reality. The insanity of reality.

On Monday morning, Mrs. Crawford stood in the doorway, looking at her daughter. She watched the still form for a few minutes before making her decision. She shook Justine's shoulder gently. "Wake up, Justine. You need to get ready for school."

Justine blocked the stabbing rays of light with her blanket. "I'm not going. I'm tired. Please let me sleep," she mumbled, sounding drugged.

Mrs. Crawford left the room and made a phone call. Two hours later, she shook Justine again. "Time to get up, honey. We're going to see Dr. Wilson."

"I don't want to go, Mom," Justine protested. "It's not Thursday."

"Come, on. Get up." Mrs. Crawford pushed and pulled, until she got her up. "What do you want to wear?"

"I don't care."

"Justine, you always care."

"I don't care."

Mrs. Crawford pulled out Justine's ugliest shirt and a pair of scrudgy pants as a test. Justine didn't even complain. Mrs. Crawford tried to feed her breakfast, but Justine gagged on the food.

"Justine, you haven't eaten much to speak of in three days."

"I'm fasting," Justine said sarcastically.

Dr. Wilson looked very concerned when Mrs. Crawford escorted drooping Justine into the room.

"How long has she been like this?"

"Since Friday."

"What triggered it?"

"A phone call from Kerry's mother."

Dr. Wilson looked at Justine. "Talk to me, Justine."

Justine shook her head.

"Tell me about the phone call," he demanded.

A gigantic sigh preceded her story. "It's not fair, Dr. Wilson. Nothing will ever be right again. It's not worth going on. It's not worth getting up in the morning."

Dr. Wilson motioned for Mrs. Crawford to sit in a chair. He sat on the couch with Justine and held her hand. "No, Justine. Nothing will ever be right again. And it isn't worth getting up in the morning to face all this sadness. Not right now. But if you stay in bed, the sadness will take over. If you get up, force yourself to get up, in spite of the unfairness of it all, you will win."

"I don't want to win right now, Dr. Wilson. I only want to go to sleep and forget it all."

Dr. Wilson took Justine into the waiting room under the watchful eye of the secretary. He went back into his office and sat on the edge of his desk, facing Mrs. Crawford.

"Justine is very depressed. It is part of the overwhelming grief she is experiencing. But we mustn't ignore it, or she may get suicidal also."

A frightened look crossed Mrs. Crawford's face. She glanced at the door leading to the waiting room.

"A young man from her school committed suicide last night." Dr. Wilson wiped his brow, sitting heavily in his chair. "Sometimes one suicide opens the door for others in the same city. It's like the first suicide gives permission for others. We call these cluster suicides. For this reason, I want to give you a list of the warning signs of suicide. I want you to clear your house of anything dangerous, or lock it up. Stay with her. Get her to exercise . . . walk with her. Take her places, but not places where everyone is having a wonderful time. That will only make her more depressed. Keep her talking. About Kerry, especially. Get her to remember the good times, the bad times, Kerry's good points, her weak points. If she has any friends you can count on, call on them too.

"Take her someplace different. To the mountains, the beach, take her with the family and maybe include a friend for the overnight outing."

He turned his chair to the file cabinet and opened a drawer. He pulled out a sheet of paper. "Here's a list of the warning signs of suicide. I think she'll be okay, but you need to be aware, in case she isn't."

Mrs. Crawford thanked him, then went to the waiting room to get Justine. Slumped in the chair, her face down, and fists resting on her cheeks, she looked lost, and forlorn.

"Honey, let's go," Mrs. Crawford said, touching her daughter's arm. Justine rose and went with her.

At home, Mrs. Crawford let Justine go back to bed. She sat at the kitchen table with her list, and a cup of tea.

Before she read it, she considered Dr. Wilson's suggestion that Justine come in twice a week until the depression had passed. Mrs. Crawford worried about Justine, and wondered how they would ever be able to pay for it all. When she finished reading the list, she decided it didn't matter how much it cost. Justine's help was more important than anything else.

Her list read:

Clues to Presuicidal Behavior

Withdrawal.

Violent behavior.

Feelings of being unwanted, especially felt by children during a divorce.

General physical complaints.

Inability to concentrate on manageable tasks.

Sleeping too much or too little, or at strange hours.

Disregard for safety, demonstrated by fast driving, dangerous sports.

A noticeable increase or decrease in the amount of food consumed.

Quick changes in personality—from outgoing to withdrawn, shy to gregarious.

Lack of interest in the future.

Loss: of a friend, a pet, a parent.

Apathy about appearance, hobbies, sleep, food, etc.

She put her hand to her forehead. The list went on. [Complete list of suicide symptoms and verbal clues listed at the end of the book.] She felt relieved and frightened at the same time. So much of the list was not Justine. But some was. She was glad to have it. Glad to know what to look for.

❧ 17 ❧

❧**M**rs. Crawford called the school, and told them Justine would not be back for a week or more. She then called and canceled her obligations, her mind filling with ideas the whole time.

Tuesday morning, she forced Justine out of bed. Justine glared at her from red, swollen eyes. "Mom, I'm not going anywhere," she protested.

"We're going to the beach."

"I don't want to go to the beach."

"You love the beach. It's warm. You can get an early start on your tan."

"I don't love the beach anymore, and tans are stupid."

"Are you putting on your bathing suit alone, or do I have to do it?"

"I'll do it."

147

Justine sat with her head against the car window, her hand playing with the door handle. Mrs. Crawford looked out of the side of her eye to be sure the door had been locked.

They put their towels on the warm sand, and Justine dropped on hers, ready for a nap.

"Oh, no you don't. We're going for a walk."

"Mom!"

Mrs. Crawford grabbed Justine's hand. "Let's go."

Justine's feet dragged in the sand. She let the water swirl around her ankles, and her thoughts flow back and forth like the sea.

"Kerry," Mrs. Crawford whispered. "Look at all you're missing."

"Kerry can't hear you, Mom." Justine spoke out into the waves. "She's dead."

She turned and started to walk through the water. The water washed her feet, stung her legs, refreshed her mind.

Each day, her mother chose something else to do. Somewhere else to go. They browsed the antique stores, strolled Ocean Front Walk in Venice. They spent a day in Palm Springs, and one in the mountains. Each day, Justine found it easier to get out of bed. Life hurt so bad she couldn't cry. It hurt so bad, she couldn't think. But the days with her mom soothed her.

They began to talk about Kerry. They asked why until their throats ached. They remembered the joy, the angry tears, and fights they had. They slogged through their guilt of what they did do, what they didn't do, and what they could have done. They emerged weary and sad.

Sunday morning, Justine told her mom, "I still can't go to church. I think I'd scream at the teacher."

Mrs. Crawford looked down at her new peach shoes. "I wish I could stay with you," she confided. "But Joey needs some kind of consistency to his life. And I think your dad is tired of covering for me. He understands, but he needs a break from the load too."

Justine smiled. "Thanks, Mom."

"Are you sure you'll be okay?"

She shrugged her shoulders. "I guess I'll cry. Maybe I'll sing, or go for a walk. Up to the park, maybe, and sit in the place where Kerry and I were pinned Girl Scouts."

"That sounds terrific. I love you, Justine."

Justine swallowed hard, and returned to her room.

As the weeks went by, Justine felt a little better about her life. But the hurt, the pain, she wondered if it would ever go away. She wondered if she could ever stop crying. She still hated to get up in the morning, still hated to make even the smallest decisions.

Two weeks ago, her mother had made her go back to work. At the time, she hated her mother for it. Now she was glad. It helped her keep busy, so she didn't have to think so hard about Kerry, or not having anything to do.

Packages with umbrellas, silver wedding bells, and congratulations piled high around her. She worked fast and sure, listening to the idle talk of the customers. The McLarens, she heard, bought Sheila a crystal cake dish for her wedding present, while the Rosenthals purchased a whole place setting of her china. Then Mrs. Gilroy tiptoed over to Justine's booth to ask what the McLarens and the Rosenthals had bought.

Mrs. Laskey came and scolded her for not being happy. "It's no fun to buy gifts here anymore, Justine. You used to make this booth shine with your smile. Now all you do is look serious. You're too young to be serious."

Justine looked at her with blank eyes. "Yes, Mrs. Laskey."

"I suppose this is all because of that Reynolds girl's foolishness. No use wasting tears on someone mentally ill. Stupid, that's what it was."

Justine wished she could close her ears. She wished she could tell the old biddy to shut up. She bit her bottom lip, her eyes welling up with tears. She finished wrapping Mrs. Laskey's package and excused herself to the rest room. On the way, she grabbed her purse and pulled out a little note-book.

In the rest room, she wrote out her anger at Mrs. Laskey, and wrote three questions to ask Dr. Wilson.

1. Was Kerry crazy, mentally sick?
2. Was Kerry stupid?
3. Why do I still hurt so bad? Shouldn't I be over this by now?

Justine wiped the corners of her eyes, washed her hands, and returned to her post. She felt much better for the thoughts she wrote, but she still couldn't smile at the cus-tomers. She worked and spoke extra polite to make up for it. But even trying her hardest, she couldn't smile.

Mr. Kelly had promised her a full-time job as a salesgirl come summer, and Justine didn't want to jeopardize that opportunity.

Sometimes, as Justine wrapped a package, she thought about what life experiences Kerry would never have. She would never graduate, Justine thought as she wrapped a graduation gift. She would never get married, or have chil-dren. No wedding or baby shower. No more birthday gifts. Her mother. . . .

Justine grabbed her purse and checked how much money she had. Not much, but she'd get paid after work today. As she wrapped more packages, she mentally went over each item in the store, until she found the perfect thing.

She carried her two wrapped packages home in a large sack, hiding one in her closet, and setting the other on the kitchen table. She sat down and stared at it a few moments, then called her mother in.

Mrs. Crawford looked at the package. "What's this?"

"It's a Mother's Day present."

"Mother's Day isn't until next Sunday."

"I know, Mom. This is for Kerry's mom."

Mrs. Crawford hugged Justine.

Justine looked at the present. "I thought that Kerry would have wanted me to do this. I mean, her mom doesn't have anyone else to give her a present. And besides, she's been almost a mom to me. Can you mail it for me?"

"Of course, Justine."

Justine felt her heart smile. She couldn't join it yet. But the ugly, dry surface of her heart had cracked.

***

What a strange quiz, Justine thought as she sucked on the end of her pen. Mr. Rodell was known for his strange assignments for senior English, but this one took the cake.

"Write a one-page essay on an emotion. Describe what that emotion feels like." He grinned after he gave the assignment—a challenging look in his eye.

Justine didn't feel like writing anything, much less write something on an emotion. Love? No, everyone would write on that. She didn't know the first thing about love. She'd blown it with Kerry. She'd fail that for sure.

Anger? No, she might explode all over the classroom. Frustration? Happiness? That's a joke. Happiness died some weeks ago. She'd forgotten what it felt like. Good grief!

Grief. That's it!

Staring at the corner of the room didn't help give her any ideas. She wrote her name in the upper right-hand corner of the page, period number, date. Still no ideas. With fifteen minutes class time left to go, she decided she'd better start writing, no matter what came out.

How do you describe grief? How can you explain the feelings of sadness mixed with real and true physical pain? You don't really see things, what's going on around you. You can drive somewhere and never know how you got there, and wonder how many red lights you missed or people you almost hit.

You can walk and not hear people speak to you. You can watch TV and never see one minute of it.

The mingled mess goes on and on, never letting up so you can catch a breath or enjoy a smile. And laugh? Did I ever laugh? What does it feel like to laugh? To be free of this pain and sadness?

One day, I noticed I didn't hurt so bad. I celebrated. The next day, it hurt worse than ever. Everything that happens to you is somehow related to the grief—at least your mind makes it so.

But goodness knows, no one can ever describe grief. I can never tell you what it feels like. You will only have to experience it yourself, to understand the heart-wrenching agony. I hope you never have to feel it. No, I take that back. I hope you do. Then we will truly be friends. Brothers in the land of grief, who touch each other, as no one else can.

"Time's up; pass the papers forward, please."

Justine reluctantly passed her paper forward. She wasn't pleased with it at all. No words could ever express how she felt. She should have chosen another topic.

***

Mr. Rodell leaned back against his desk, a stack of papers in his hand. "Well, class. You did a fine job on your little quiz yesterday. As expected, most of you wrote on love, without knowing what real love is." He lifted his eyebrow as the class tittered. "I want to read a couple of the better ones to you, then I will read one written on an emotion I must honestly say, I hadn't anticipated."

Dropping her head onto her arms, Justine blocked out the giggles and groans as Mr. Rodell read about love. She wondered what she could do to soften the ache inside, where she could go to get rid of it. Dr. Wilson said she could run away anywhere, but it wouldn't take away the ache. It was too deep, and a part of her. She would have to learn to live with it. She would have to learn to make it a memory, to store it with all memories, good and bad.

"Grief," Mr. Rodell began.

Justine's head popped up, then she slunk down in her chair. Her face felt hot, and she dropped her eyes. Midway through, she looked up. It didn't sound so bad as he read it. She looked around the class. No one laughed; everyone seemed interested.

"I'm giving this paper an *A*," Mr. Rodell said when he finished. "It shows insight and honesty. I don't think I could get a good picture of what grief is by reading it, but I do get a clear picture of the person who is experiencing it. Thank you, Justine."

To her horror, the whole class turned to look at her. Most of the class looked on with kindness, others with curiosity.

***

"Oh, Jack. You ought to go see Dr. Wilson. He really helps."

Jack stared at his toes. "Mom thinks that God is enough."

"Doesn't God expect us to go to doctors when we are physically sick? Don't we go to dentists when our teeth are damaged? We go talk to the pastor when our relationship with God is out of whack. So why not go to a professional counselor when our emotions are sick?"

Jack shrugged his shoulders. "I want to go see somebody," he admitted. "Sometimes I feel like I'm going to explode, and other times I feel like I'm going to fall apart. But most of the time I feel like I can't go on."

Justine closed her locker and leaned against it. Her eyes lit up. "I've got it! The school is calling in a couple of special counselors to talk about suicide next week. Maybe you could talk to one of them."

Jack looked at her, his face dull. "You really think it will help?"

"Without Dr. Wilson, I might still be in bed sleeping all day, and unable to face the world."

Jack looked incredulous. "Don't you hurt anymore?"

Justine's eyes filled with tears. As she spoke, they poured down her face. She buried her face in Jack's chest. "Oh, Jack. I don't know if I'll ever stop hurting."

Jack put one limp arm around her. She stepped back and wiped her eyes. "I'd have gone crazy if I didn't talk to someone about it. Someone who knew something. You know? Talking to friends didn't help. They don't want to hear about it anymore."

Jack nodded his understanding. "I guess I'll go make an appointment with a counselor. It can't hurt."

***

Justine didn't know if she could go through with it. She had no idea why she agreed to speak to the school about Kerry's suicide. Mr. Rodell had recommended her to the principal, and encouraged her to do it. *I am crazy*, she thought. *Funny how* crazy *means something different nowadays.* Crazy *used to mean fun. Now it means CRAZY.*

She only did it because she was quite sure it was something God wanted her to do. She had to stop the craziness Kerry had started. Two boys in her school had killed themselves in the seven weeks since Kerry. It was like an epidemic. She didn't have the answers, but she had a little strength. A little something that might help.

The last time she had been backstage like this was when

she and Kerry had sung. She would get no standing ovation this time. Tears started to come, and she wanted to push them back, but knew she shouldn't. She listened to the special counselors speak, her body shaking with nerves.

Justine cleared her throat as she stepped out on the stage. She heard a few sniffles from somewhere in the darkened audience. Her heart pumped so hard, she could hear it in her ears. She grabbed onto the sides of the large wooden podium, holding on for support.

"As you know," she began softly, "my friend Kerry killed herself. I can't imagine her stopping what was going to be a rich and full life. But I guess she thought it had stopped being rich and full, and that it would never be so again."

Justine wiped her eyes, and looked down at the podium, at the initials and names carved in the top. She traced one. "Just because she killed herself, and she's now getting all this attention, doesn't give any of you the right or the freedom to do the same. I guess Bob James and Eddie Stanford thought they had the right to kill themselves too. I didn't know them so I can't say much about that. I only know how I felt about my very best friend.

"Just a couple of weeks after she swallowed all those pills, a letter came for her in the mail. It was a letter that fulfilled all her dreams. Listen."

Choking on the words, Justine read the answer to a dream. Her voice broke, the tears coming in little sobs. Justine tried to control herself, and spoke each word alone. When she finished reading, she looked out into the crowd.

"All she needed to do was hold on for a few more days. Maybe you hurt so bad you cry every day. Maybe you hurt so bad you know it can never get any better. Well I want you to hold on. Hold on, and cry. Hold on and talk to someone who can help you.

"I know most of you don't know I've had to see a counselor. I thought a lot about killing myself too. I didn't think that life could be worth living if such a talented, terrific person saw no other way out but death. After that letter came, I crawled into bed, and never wanted to face the world again. I almost offed myself too, you guys, so I know there are those of you thinking about it.

"Please stop, and remember Kerry's letter. My God is big enough to hold you, and hold you until the hurting stops, no matter how long that takes. Just talk to Him. He'll hear you. There is always something to live for. Thank you."

She turned and almost bumped into Jack. He squeezed her arm before taking over the podium. Justine heard the tears in his voice as he dismissed the kids back to their classes. Justine heard someone blow his nose. A male voice started to hoot about something, and someone else shouted, "Cut it out, Greg." Then all was silent again, except for the scuffling feet, and the theater seats being folded up as people filed by.

***

"Doctor, what would have helped Kerry?" Justine asked the following day.

"I hate these questions because the answer is different with each person. The basic answer seems only as if I am advertising. But truly, counseling is the best help."

"Why counseling?" Justine asked, cocking her head.

Dr. Wilson smiled. "How has counseling helped you?"

Justine pulled her brows together. "It makes me think. It opens my eyes, to get a broader picture of life. I never knew how narrow my vision was before—like looking through a telescope. I missed what was going on around me, and saw only one thing that was always magnified."

"Right," answered Dr. Wilson. "Kerry needed someone to help her see what was beyond the hopelessness of today. She needed to see how many people loved her and cared for her. She needed someone to help her list her options, then act on them."

Leaning back in his chair, Dr. Wilson rested his feet on his desk. "It is possible she had physical reasons for her depression. There are chemical imbalances in the brain that can create depression. It could have been hormonal imbalances. And it could have been her circumstances. We don't know, because we weren't able to talk with her about it.

"An untrained person cannot know which of the reasons I've stated causes another person's depression."

"Would a suicide hot line have been able to help?"

"Oh, my, yes. They are such wonderful people. They are willing to listen and talk. Often a suicidal person needs someone to listen, without making judgments or making silly statements like, 'It's not that bad,' or, 'You'll get over it,' or even, 'You think you've got it bad, what about. . . .' "

Justine sat up straight in her chair. "That's what Kerry used to say. She said it wasn't fair to get depressed, because somebody always had it worse than she."

The doctor shook his head. "Each hurt we have, hurts. We should never minimize our hurts because someone else has a worse hurt. Pain is pain, hurt is hurt. We can't compare."

"Why do I hurt so bad still? Shouldn't I be over this by now?"

"No, Justine. I would be surprised if you no longer hurt a year from now. This kind of pain never completely goes away."

"A lady said Kerry was stupid. Was she?"

"Like so many people who hurt deeply, they don't know what is wrong or how to get help. So they do something that shouts for attention. A cry for help. 'Somebody help me,' their actions say. But too often, no one hears."

Justine sank into the back of the couch. "So you don't think she meant to kill herself?"

Dr. Wilson sadly shook his head. "That's the true tragedy of suicide. Most people don't really want to die. They only want out of a desperate and endless situation."

"She wasn't crazy, then?"

"No, Justine. She wasn't crazy. Only very sad."

❧ 18 ❧

❧The bedroom door was shut, but it didn't shut out the noise from within. Joey ran to get Justine, grabbing her hand and pulling her to the room. His frightened face looked up at her. "Daddy's crying. Why would Daddy cry?"

Justine stood in the hallway, listening, feeling guilty for eavesdropping.

"Sandra, it's not like she was a stranger. I watched her grow up," her father said through his tears.

"It seems like only yesterday they were flying around the room together acting out 'Lonely Goatherd' from *The Sound of Music*," her mother added with a sigh.

"Or playing Wonder Woman. Oh, Sandra. I miss Kerry so much, I don't think I can stand it."

At this, her father broke into heavy sobs. Justine took Joey's hand and led him to his room. She shoved aside the pile of stuffed animals and dirty clothes to sit on his bed. Joey picked up his Cabbage Patch Kid and hugged it tight.

"Why are they crying, Justine?"

Wrapping her arms around him, she pressed his head against her shoulder. She didn't know how to explain without crying herself. "They're crying because they're sad that Kerry died," she began.

"I'm sad about that, too," Joey said in a soft voice. "I thought maybe she could be my sister someday. She didn't laugh at Mister Rogers like you do. Why did she have to die?"

Justine bit her lip and looked at the ceiling. "She didn't, Joey. That's why we are very sad."

Joey pushed out his bottom lip. He squeezed his doll with all his might. "But I don't like Daddy or Mommy to cry."

"I don't either. But it's okay to cry." Tears spilled down Justine's face. "It's really okay to cry," she whispered.

***

Claudia worked Justine harder than ever. "If you're going to have a song of yours and Kerry's out in the world, you'd better work hard. You are going to be in demand one of these days."

"I am?" Justine asked, incredulous.

"Sure." Claudia looked up from the piano as the door to the studio opened. "And here is someone else who is already in demand."

Justine turned to see Mark peeking in. Claudia swept over to him. "Mark, how nice to see you! Do you know Justine? She has just signed a contract to have her song on Shelly Grammercy's new album!"

The shy look left Mark's face, and an appreciative one

took its place. "Congratulations. I admire anyone who can write music. I can sing halfway decent, but I can't write a word." He shook her hand, and then the shy look came again.

"I'm sorry, am I early?" he asked. "Did I disrupt your lesson?"

Glancing at the clock, Justine shook her head. "No, it's over." She waved good-bye to Claudia and hustled out the door.

That night, as she tried to study for her History final, she got a phone call.

"Mark? Mark who?" she asked, her mind fuzzy from studying.

"Mark from Claudia's. I saw you this afternoon."

"Oh, yeah."

"You left your tape at Claudia's, and I told Claudia I live close by and could bring it over to you."

"You don't have to do that, but it would be nice." Justine wanted to be friendly, but the part Kerry killed with her death couldn't seem to come alive.

Mark cleared his throat. "I, uh . . . I thought I could bring it by on Friday. Then if you wanted to, we could go to the Diana Ross concert at the Greek."

"You have tickets?"

"Yeah."

"They've been sold out since the second day of sales. How long did you wait in line for them?"

There was a long pause, and Justine wondered if he was still there. "I didn't," came the quiet answer.

"Then how—"

"My agent has some connection. They're front-section seats too. I've been to other concerts and sat in the same seats. I've never enjoyed concerts so much as when I can get these tickets."

Justine liked his manner. He didn't sound pushy, nervous, or even bragging. He was stating the truth in his shy way. "Okay. That would be very nice."

***

Mark's ancient Datsun jerked along the road, the muffler rumbling so loudly, Justine could hardly hear him talk . . . which wasn't often anyway. She wondered how she'd get through an evening with someone so shy, when she didn't feel much like acting happy. She couldn't play the game anymore. The game of pretending you're having fun even if you were not. Like the night she went out with Larry. She could laugh, and talk a lot, and make her own fun. But Kerry's cloud hung over everything she did now.

Mark had been right. The seats were in the perfect spot. They could see the stage without looking at the performer's feet. They would be able to see her face and expressions.

When they had been seated, Mark turned to Justine, looking straight into her eyes. "You don't have to act happy or anything. Claudia told me what happened."

Justine dropped her eyes, a little angry at Claudia for revealing her secret. *He's only brought me because he feels sorry for me.*

"I know it takes a long time to get over feeling hurt when somebody close to you dies. My dad died a little over a year ago in a car accident. I still have trouble feeling happy sometimes."

Justine looked up at him, a tiny smile on her face. "Thanks, Mark."

Mark looked away, embarrassed. His statement opened the door for Justine to feel free to just talk.

"What did you mean when you said 'your agent'?" she asked him a few moments later.

Mark's face changed to an even-deeper shade of red. "Oh, I shouldn't have said that."

"No, tell me. I'm curious. I know you aren't bragging."

Mark sighed, then clasped his hands together. "I sing background for a couple of radio commercials. Not much, but it's a start."

"Do you really? For what commercials?"

"A gum commercial, and a soda pop. I'll be doing the jingle for a radio station next week. That will be my biggest job so far."

"What do you want to do with your music?"

"I just want to do backgrounds on albums. That's my goal. The pay is good, the pressure small. What do you want to do with your singing?"

"I don't know, Mark. I don't know what I want for the future at all."

"That will come," he said smiling. "Indecision is a part of pain. Choices for the future come with healing. Don't push it. You'll know."

The lights dimmed, and the warm-up group came out on stage. Justine wondered at Mark's wisdom, forgetting about it when the dynamic presence of Diana Ross took over the stage.

Justine made herself very busy over the next weeks. Finals, working, graduation preparations, all filled her time. She spent most of her time working hard at her singing. She had no goal to aim for, but she knew the goal would come.

She didn't tell anyone at school about Mark. It didn't seem fair that she could enjoy moments of life, when Kerry had taken hers. Kerry saw ugliness, where Justine had seen joy. The whole thing didn't make sense and was too confusing. So many times, she stopped a smile from coming. She didn't think it fair to Kerry for her to smile. Pain never left, but sometimes she could smile through the pain. Oh, it was all too confusing.

In the grove, she tried to talk to her friends about it all.

"Justine, can't you forget about it?"

"You're so morbid. Always talking about Kerry."

"I'm sick of hearing about it. If you can't be happy, then don't come around here."

She often sat on the farthest bench, in the farthest corner, away from her friends. She couldn't wait until school ended in only a couple of weeks.

***

Jack sat in the counselor's office, picking at the corner of the desk. It was his fourth visit in as many weeks. Each time he went in, he felt guilty for going behind his parents' backs, for doing something they thought was wrong. He felt stupid that he, as a man, could not cope with this on his own. He almost didn't go, but each time, Justine caught him in the hallway and made sure he went.

When he left the counselor's office, he often felt raw and bleeding, but also a taste of hope. He got a C on one final, to make sure he wouldn't be asked to do a graduation speech. He couldn't give a speech of hope and encouragement to his class. He had nothing to give anyone.

He and Justine went to the movies a couple of times together, but Jack always felt guilty. He wondered if people thought he really didn't love Kerry. That one girl was as good as another. He had only gone with Justine because she really wanted to see the movie and didn't have anyone to go with. He wouldn't do it again, he decided. He wouldn't give people a chance to talk. His loyalty was to Kerry.

He sat in his room one afternoon, the stereo cranked up to level five. His mom came in and turned the volume down. "Jack," she said, her voice stern and commanding. "You have not yet sent in your final papers for UCLA. You've been accepted at one of the finest schools in Southern California, and you won't act responsibly."

She put her hands on her wide hips, and tapped her toe.

"I want you to fill out the papers and send them in tomorrow. Do you hear me?"

Jack kept his back to her. "I don't need the papers. I'm not going," he said flatly.

"You most certainly *are* going."

"I'm not going. I can't concentrate. Every time I have a quiet moment I think about Kerry. I'm not going to school in the fall."

"Your father and I will not have a bum in this house. Your sister will be graduating with honors this year from UCLA," she told him as if he hadn't heard it a hundred times already. "Your brother is on the dean's list for the second year in a row. You will go, and you will do as well."

"Good for them. I won't go. I will fail if I go. And I will not be a bum." Jack turned in his chair and cranked the stereo back up. His mother "hmmphed" and left the room. Jack didn't care.

19

The seniors of Central High stood in line, alternating boy/girl. Each boy looked handsome in his tuxedo, each girl very pretty in her white dress, a bouquet of red carnations in her arms. The grass of the stadium had been decorated with tissue-paper flowers by the junior class, in the design of the senior-class emblem.

Parents sat in the stands, mothers rolling hankies in their hands, fathers joking easily with the folks around them, everyone bragging about the accomplishments of their children.

Justine felt so alone in line. She had asked Jack if they could be next to each other. It hurt when he said no. He had acted so strange lately. He almost ran when he saw her approaching in the hall.

She stood with Larry on one side, a peach-fuzz-faced stranger on the other. Larry spent most of his time talking with Eileen. Every time Justine looked at Peach Fuzz, he grinned, encouraging friendship Justine wanted to ignore.

"Pomp and Circumstance" filled the air. A sad sound. A sound of finality, of this portion of life that had come to an end. The students' procession filed slowly into the seats of honor.

Boring speeches followed, and awards were presented. Names were called for fake diplomas given out. A moment of silence was observed when they came to Kerry's name. And then the procedure continued.

Justine was glad when it was all over. The time of her life. The time she had worked for all her life. Over. Ending in a puff of time under a hot, smoggy, spring sky. She sat in the slippery metal chair, straight and tall. Thinking, remembering. Each year of school passed in her memories. The years of kindergarten, playing, resting, eager for a turn to play an instrument at music time. Then first grade, molding rabbits out of clay. . . .

With the memories came tears. Nothing fun could be experienced again. Nothing bad could be done over, and the worst part of it all seemed like a nightmare.

The ceremony ended with cheers, flowers, and Ping-Pong balls tossed into the air. Justine stood in the shower of junk, empty.

Her friends hugged her, telling her how much her friendship meant, and how they would all keep in touch. Drugheads, nerds, and flits also came to her, and told her how they appreciated her. She was different and accepted everyone. None of the kindness soaked into the place where she needed it the most. It began to roll off her back. *I wanted to be like Kerry. And now I am. What hell she must have lived in.*

She turned down several party offers, refusing even to go

to grad night at Disneyland. Her mother wanted to have a celebration at home with all the local relatives and some close family friends. Justine declined as politely as she could. Her mother understood, and hid her disappointment.

Justine went instead to a quiet dinner with Mark at the Sheraton Premiere Hotel at Universal Studios.

Still dressed in white, she tried to act elegant and sophisticated to match her surroundings. Everything had been decorated in mauve and cream, the new favorite colors of interior designers. The restaurant hardly looked like one. It sat off to one side in the enormous lobby. Mark had requested a quiet table—one with a sofalike bench so they could be seated next to each other.

They didn't need menus, for Mark had ordered for both of them ahead of time. The waitress brought a bottle of sparkling cider in a champagne bucket, pouring them each a glass as if it were fine wine.

Mark lifted Justine's drooping chin, so he could look into her eyes. "It's been a hard day, hasn't it?"

Justine nodded, her eyes filling with tears. She dabbed at them with a napkin. "This is supposed to be such a happy day . . . a day to remember. I hated it. It wasn't at all what I expected, and. . . ." Her voice faded.

"My graduation wasn't much fun either. My dad had died six months before. It took all the joy out of the day. I kept hoping I'd turn around to see him in the audience, waving proudly at me, jumping into the aisle, popping off pictures and embarrassing the heck out of me. I had nothing to look forward to anymore."

Justine appreciated the understanding. It lightened her load to know someone else had felt the same. She wasn't weird.

"I also got an award in music. There was a big dinner for all the award winners. They said lots of wonderful things about why I deserved the award. My dad missed that too. He was the one responsible for helping me in my music. He would have been so proud."

"Was he a musician?"

Mark laughed a little, shaking his head. "No. Dad was a jock. He won every kind of award for football through school. He was so disappointed at first that his son wouldn't follow in his footsteps. When he found out I loved music, he thought he had some sort of whoosh on his hands. He got used to my music, realized I was as much a man as he, and became my biggest supporter. He encouraged me at every step. He helped me look at both sides of all decisions, making certain I was doing and choosing the best for me."

"No wonder it hurt so bad when he died."

"It still does."

The soup arrived, and they ate quietly, enjoying the harpist who played her music in the background. The next courses came in slow succession. Justine felt better with each one.

"Mark, you seem so much older than me, instead of just one year."

Mark smiled. "Thanks, I don't feel like it. Really, though, I think a lot has to do with my dad."

Justine nodded. "I know what you mean. Somehow I could not go to grad night, and join in all the silliness. I'm not trying to be above my friends or anything, it's just that I've left so many of my young thoughts behind in the last three months."

"You'll enjoy being silly again. It will take time. It will also mean more to laugh. When someone really feels pain, laughter has a different meaning."

Two hours of eating and talking passed in soft comfort. The waiter set a piece of chocolate mousse pie in front of each of them. Jack took one bite, then set his fork down. "Full?" Justine asked him.

"No," he said, wiping his mouth with his napkin. "I just can't wait any longer. I've saved the two best things for last. They're sort of graduation presents."

"Oh, boy. What?"

"First, my agent wants to talk to you about representing you. I sneaked one of your tapes out of your room with your mom's help. I played it for him, and told him about your song with Shelly Grammercy. He thinks he can line you up with some good work."

Justine's eyes grew wide. "You're kidding."

Mark shook his head. "I'm not kidding. I made an appointment on Wednesday after my voice lesson. You can wait and hear my lesson, and then we'll go together. His office is near Claudia's."

"Oh, Mark," she whispered. "This is the best graduation present. I hope I do okay. My voice can be so awful. And what will I wear?"

Mark laughed and put his hand on hers. "Now, for the other graduation present." He pulled a small wrapped box from his pocket, pushed her plate aside, and set it in front of her.

Justine opened the card first. She read it, then dropped it on the table. "I can't, Mark." She pushed the present back to him. "I can't promise you I'll be there for you."

"This doesn't mean get married, Justine. It only means I want to commit myself to you, to let you know I'm there for you. I wanted to know if you could do the same for me."

Justine hung her head. "Mark, right now all I can do is hold on. That's all I have energy for. And holding on means working at Kelly's full time, and singing. Hold on and survive, and try to figure out everything else."

"I'm sorry, Justine. I should know that. It's just that I care so much for you. I will still make my commitment to you. And I want you to have this gift, even if I never see you again."

"Mark," she said gently. "You are so sweet. I want so much to see you again and again. I simply can't promise anyone anything. I have to leave myself free to think. It takes so much of my time these days."

"I know. Here. Open this before I go nuts."

The wrapping came off, revealing a tiny black box. Opening its hinged cover, Justine gasped. "It's beautiful, Mark." She slipped on the ring with six little diamonds surrounding a small ruby.

Mark put his arm around her and kissed her cheek. "It's for someone who is as beautiful on the outside as she is on the inside."

Justine blushed. "Don't get weird on me."

Justine crawled in bed that night, twirling her new ring around and around. She began to cry, her small tears turning into big ones, then to sobs. "Oh, God, Kerry has missed out on so much. And it's only been three months. What other zillions of things is she going to miss? Even if it took a year for things to get better for her, or two. What is that in an eighty-year lifetime? What is that compared to the celebration that goes on much of life? The first snow, the first spring flowers, the first beach trip of the summer, the first harvest, or fall colors?"

Pulling her pillow over head so her parents wouldn't hear and come in, she sobbed into the bed. "Dear God, why couldn't Kerry hold on? Why couldn't she reach out to You? You are such a big God. Thank You for holding me. Thank You for my mother, who took me to Dr. Wilson. Thank You for helping me through that man, God. Thanks for being there."

As she opened her wounded heart to God, He began a new healing. She had not talked to Him in so long, and now

He was right there. Waiting to be her friend again. She saw how He had been there even when she thought He had forgotten she existed. All the people who had been God with skin on to her. Loving, caring, letting her cry.

She fell asleep with a sad peace.

❧ 20 ❧

❧Justine nibbled her croissant sandwich, then sipped her iced tea. She smiled at Jack. "It's been a long time, Jack."

"It just seems that way. Pain stretches time."

"It's been nine months. So much has happened."

Jack popped a chunk of warm, honey-buttered cornbread into his mouth. He wanted to say something but wasn't sure if he could.

"Do you think you'll ever get married, Jack?"

Jack signaled for the waitress and ordered another glass of iced tea.

"You're stalling, Jack."

Jack smiled. "You bet. You don't think I want to get caught in that one, do you?"

"I don't mean to catch you. I was just curious."

Jack looked down at his plate. "I know. It's a painful question." He pushed his plate forward, and leaned on the table. "I know I will. But it won't be for a long time. I knew Kerry was the one. And I don't want to go looking for another Kerry. I'd only ruin myself and the poor girl who couldn't be someone else. I guess what I'm trying to say is that I'm going to let time do some more healing before I even think about dating again."

The waitress set the wet glass in front of him, and removed the empty one. He thanked her, then looked at Justine. "You know, Justine. I once told Kerry that two thinkers understand each other. But I never did understand why she did that. Did you?"

"No. I have some ideas about why she hurt. But never, never, could I understand why she killed herself."

"Let's change the subject," Jack suggested. "How are you?"

Justine cocked her head. "You asked that when we met here. I said fine."

"No," Jack said, shaking his head. "How *are* you?"

"I suppose okay. Sometimes I wonder if there will ever be a day when I don't hurt. Dr. Wilson assures me there will. That one day I will wake up, surprised that it has been a few days, or a week, that I haven't thought about it."

"Are you still seeing Dr. Wilson?"

"No. I stopped a couple of months ago. We thought it was time to put to practice what I've learned. I'll go back in a month to report."

"And? How are things going?"

"Okay. You know what the most important thing is that he told me?"

Jack took another bite, and shook his head.

"He said that it's a fact of life that deep pain never goes away. It only heals to a barbed memory. After some time, the barbs only hurt when you walk too close to the memory. When you see something or someone that will remind you of that pain."

Jack smiled, his face grateful. "Justine, thank you. That helps me. I was beginning to think something was wrong with me. Every time I turned around, and ran into my memories, it hurt so bad." He tossed his napkin in the air. "Hooray! I'm normal!" he said softly.

"I still think sometimes it was all a bad dream," Justine told him. "I think that Kerry will come walking back into my life, and we'll pick up our friendship where it left off." She hung her head. "And sometimes I even feel like Kerry was the dream, and she never existed. Oh, Jack. *Why?*"

"We'll never understand or stop asking why, will we?"

Justine shook her head.

"We'll never completely heal either," he added.

"No, we never will."

Silence separated them for the moment.

"Have you been going to UCLA?" Justine changed the subject.

"No. I couldn't concentrate. I only had fragmented thoughts. I've been working in a men's store, in shoes. I met terrific people, and learned a lot about life in general."

Justine grew worried. "Are you going to do that for the rest of your life?"

Jack threw back his head and laughed. *"No!* I like it, but not that much. I'm going to Cambridge in August. I'm going to study History."

"Ugh. Kerry's worst subject. My almost-worst. Why Cambridge?"

"It's far away. It's another country. Actually, it is an excellent school. But there are many excellent schools here, too. My first reason for choosing it is for its distance."

Justine leaned forward over her plate, her eyes narrowed. "Are you running away?"

"Of course," Jack said, delighted. Then he got serious.

"I'm running from the memories, but I'm also hoping to find healing in distance and a new situation. Like I said, here, I can't concentrate. I think studying and doing something I love will help me to heal. But I can't do that here. It's too close to the pain."

"I'm so glad for you, Jack. You sound so much better than the last time we talked."

"I have you to thank for that. Without your suggestion to get counseling, I don't think I would be here today."

Both finished their lunches and shoved their plates aside. The busboy was by in minutes, whisking the plates away. The waitress stopped and asked, "Pie?"

"Please."

They both ordered the fresh strawberry pie, and then continued their conversation.

"What about you, Justine? I've heard Kerry's and your songs on the radio. You must be doing something right."

Justine stirred her tea with a straw. "Our first song, sung by Shelly Grammercy, was a hit, you know. I got enough money from that to save some for school, and to make more, better-quality tapes. I've got an agent now who really knows the business. He sends my stuff to the right A & R people. As they heard the tapes, they not only liked the songs, they even liked my voice."

Jack raised his eyebrows, and Justine laughed. "Can you believe it? Anyway, they've asked me to do a background vocal on some new star's album. I've also done two background vocals for commercials."

"Terrific!" Jack said, reaching across the table to squeeze Justine's hand. "If I had known I was lunching with a star, I would have brought roses, and made you pay for lunch!"

Justine laughed. "I'm no star, Jack. But it's fun to be doing some professional singing."

"Do you want to pursue singing, cut your own album, and all that?"

"No," Justine said, her voice getting quiet. "That was Kerry's dream. Not mine. I've had to find my own dream."

"What's that?"

"You'll die laughing. I mean, here I have a chance to make gobs of bucks with singing, and I only want that to be a hobby."

"So what is it? Tell me so I can laugh. I don't do that much."

Justine sipped her tea, thanked the waitress for the pie, and dug in. "Yum. This is the best, most fattening stuff."

She wiped her mouth, and answered his question. "I'm going to go to school in the fall and become an occupational therapist."

"You're going to teach people how to do crafts?"

"Oh, it's more than that. When people get hurt in car accidents, or are dysfunctional because of strokes or disabilities, I get to teach them how to be independent."

"Sounds interesting."

"I really want to work with the kids. You know, I've been volunteering at the children's hospital, and it is the most rewarding thing I've done in my life. We have one kid, seventeen, who was hurt so bad in a car accident, they thought he'd just lie in bed for the rest of his life, dependent on others for everything."

She shoved a couple more bites of pie into her mouth before continuing.

"Well, we've taught him how to chew, and how to hold a spoon. We're teaching him how to talk. We encourage him by telling him all he can be and do with his voice."

"I don't think I've ever seen you so excited about anything before."

"I haven't been, Jack. And I do have Kerry to thank. Without our songs being on the radio, and the extra income I make singing background, I could never have gone to

179

school for this. And I never would have imagined the importance of people, if she had not killed herself."

"So are you thankful she killed herself?" Jack was not accusing, only wondering.

"Oh, no, Jack," Justine said, her eyes filling up with tears. "I could never be thankful for that. I am only thankful for the lessons God taught me through it."

"And those are?"

"The most important is the inestimable value of every life. And I'm able to help my patients see that in themselves. *They must* see that in themselves. Some have to search deeper and harder than others to find that joy and purpose—especially if they don't believe in God. I help give them something to live for."

Jack's grin seemed to cover his whole face. "Do you see what you've done?"

Justine looked confused. "No, what?"

"You've made me have hope that I will be given something special by God, too."

Justine reached across to squeeze Jack's arm. "Oh, He will, if you only ask Him to."

"I haven't kept in contact with the Reynolds," Jack confessed. "I never knew what to say. Have you heard from them?"

Justine pressed her lips together before answering. "Yes. They've never gotten over the blow. They moved back out here to be close to friends. They live in silent, separate worlds. Mrs. Reynolds takes pills all the time and refuses to talk about Kerry's death. She talks about her 'baby' from time to time, but never the teenage Kerry. Mr. Reynolds has given up trying to do well in his job and was demoted. He doesn't care, and only works because he must."

"That's terrible."

"I have begged them to get help, but they won't. They figure if they pretend it didn't happen, it will all go away. I'm scared for them. I wonder if they will cash it in someday too. I can't seem to break through that barrier. They won't even cry."

"I should go see them."

"Pray for them too. I don't know what will break through. I'm going to keep trying."

Jack looked at her. "You've grown to be quite a neat person, Justine."

"Thanks, Jack. I don't feel like it. Mark says suffering, if looked at as an opportunity for growth, can be the best character-building process."

"I don't care about character. I just want to stop hurting."

"I'm with you, Jack. But I guess trying to heal builds character without our knowing."

"You are awfully wise for almost nineteen."

"I don't try to be."

The pie finished, the plates cleared away, both ordered coffee, just to have a reason to stay longer.

"Whatever happened to Mark?" Jack asked her.

"He's still around. As a matter of fact, if you can keep a secret. . . ."

Jack nodded as Justine looked around the room, making certain no one listened. "We've been talking about getting married."

"No! When?"

"In a year, or so. It depends on my studies and his singing. We don't want to jeopardize either of our dreams. They are more important than getting married. If we think we can swing it, we will!"

Lunch ended too soon for both of them. They promised to keep in touch, and knew they would. They had a special bond no one could break. They needed each other for support, and to remember how far they had come. They hugged in the lobby of the restaurant, and said their good-byes, warm from the love and support of the friendship.

❧ 21 ❧

❧ The pen moved swiftly across the page, blopping out extra globs of ink every few words. Justine paid no attention to the globs. Thoughts raced through her mind, and she tried to keep up. So many feelings came with the thoughts. Anger, hurt, gratitude, healing, love, despair.

April 12

Dear Kerry,

It's been over a year since you died. Since you killed yourself. (I have to tell the blunt truth, or I begin to deny everything.) This has been the worst year of my life. I have never hurt so bad, or thought so hard in all my life.

Time continues to move ahead. And because of that, I

had to make a choice. Either I move ahead, or I cry forever over the best friend I've ever had.

At first, I thought if I stopped crying, that would mean I didn't really care about you or love you. But that isn't true.

What is true is that I will always miss you. I will remember what you did every time I remember the prom. I will remember every Mother's Day and Father's Day when I send your parents gifts. I will remember every September fifth, as I count how old you would have been.

I remember now, every time I hear someone else's voice sing your songs on the radio—especially the songs we wrote together.

I've been studying a little on suicide, hoping and trying to understand why you did it. I've learned so much.

Now I know it wasn't my fault. There was a whole lifetime of problems and feelings that were held together in a little pot. And in one month, too many things happened, and you let that pot get too full, and it exploded.

Sure, your mother always loved her best friend more than you, and that hurt. But you pretended it didn't.

You depended on a talent, and friends, to believe your life had purpose. And when your dreams seemed snatched away, you decided to exit.

It wasn't my fault

It wasn't anyone's fault. It was lots of problems, and no help to deal with those problems.

I'm sorry I didn't hear how loudly you cried for help. I did the best that I could at the time.

I have so many wishes. . . .

I wish you would have gotten help from a counselor, a hot line, a psychologist, or psychiatrist. They listen. They help you see more than just the box you are in. They help you see the outside.

I'm finally starting to smile freely again. I laughed *hard* the other day. Jack has just begun to be funny again. We laugh, and then we cry. We talk about you—with less anger and sadness now.

I have not betrayed your memory. Time cannot stop because you stopped in time. My life will never, ever be the same. But it will be better because I was forced by your death to take a different look at life.

Life is to celebrate, Kerry.

In the hard times we need help to make it through the fire. But when we get to the other side, and the smoke clears, there is rejoicing.

Oh, Kerry. The biggest thing you taught me is that I have something to live for. I only wish you had known that.

Emma is fine. We talk about you a lot.

I miss you, Kerry.

I love you.

FACT SHEET ON TEENAGE SUICIDE

Identifying Presuicide Symptoms

Many of the following symptoms are quite common among adolescents and are not on their own necessarily indicative of suicidal tendencies. But when several occur together or with unusual intensity, the possibility of suicide should be considered and precautions taken.

1) Rebelliousness toward authority, indicated by fighting, committing petty crimes, abusing drugs and alcohol, etc.

2) Disregard for safety, demonstrated by fast driving, dangerous sports, etc.

3) An extremely moody or withdrawn attitude that often begins even before adolescence.

4) Feelings of being unwanted, which are particularly prevalent among youngsters during a divorce.

5) Highly indirect questions about homosexuality, which may reveal the common (but mostly unfounded) fear of having that problem.

6) A noticeable increase or decrease in the amount of food consumed.

7) A new drinking habit, or excessive drinking. The person may be using alcohol to gain courage for taking his life.

8) Sleeping too much, too little, or at strange hours. Be especially aware of early waking in the morning.

9) Quick changes in personality—from outgoing to withdrawn, quiet to gregarious, thrifty to spendthrift, etc.

10) Long-term mood swings.

11) Lack of interest in the future, which may be reflected in poor grades or boredom with schoolwork.

12) Lack of friends, either by driving them off or never having had any.

13) Chronic physical complaints that are medically unexplained.

14) Possession of a gun, pills, or other means to commit suicide.

15) Loss of a parent, boyfriend or girlfriend, pet, favorite rock star, etc. Also, loss of self-esteem or a cherished ideal.

16) Apathy about appearance, hobbies, sleep, food, friends, etc.

17) Constant self-depreciation.

18) A suicide note. It is not a joke, even if the writer insists it is.

19) Apparent preparation for death by giving away favorite possessions, such as record or stamp collections, along with verbal clues such as, "I won't be needing this anymore."

20) Good-byes said in final terms: "If I don't see you again, thanks for everything." "If anything ever happens to me, don't blame yourself."

21) Other verbal clues: "I've had it." "I've lived long enough." "They won't have me to kick around anymore." "Do you believe in reincarnation?" "Do you know the procedure for donating your eyes after death?" etc.

Reaching Out to Prevent Suicide

Recognizing the symptoms provides a platform to work from, but it is still necessary to identify the causes of despair and provide concern, hope, and friendship. The following guidelines are designed to expedite that process.

1) In a sensitive manner, mention having noticed signs of difficulties and ask for an explanation. If the response indicates a serious problem, ask, "Have you had thoughts of harming yourself/committing suicide?" Be forthright in discussing the subject, indicate real interest, and don't be deterred by joking or mild hostility.

2) If he has thought about suicide, ask how he would do it. If there is a specific plan, suicide may be imminent. Also, the more deadly the method, the greater the danger. However, if a youth believes a less effective method is deadly, his threat should still be taken seriously.

3) Ascertain whether the adolescent has access to the means he has chosen. If he carries a deadly instrument with him, he may be very close to committing suicide.

4) Attempt to determine how upset the teenager is. As a general rule, the more disturbed, the more likely he will act upon his plans. Previous suicide attempts or a suicide in his family are additional warning signals.

5) Once you assess the severity of the problem, pray for the youngster. Better yet, pray *with* him.

6) Listen and try to understand. Be hopeful without being unrealistic.

7) Gently examine the causes of distress. Help him see clearly both his problems and available resources.

8) Discuss the reality of death and dispel any romantic illusions the adolescent may have about it.

9) Try convincing the person to surrender whatever instrument he intends to use in the suicide. Such people often have a fascination with the means of death and may be dissuaded if they do not have access to it. But even if the person relinquishes his gun, bottle of pills, etc., he may have another method in reserve. Be especially aware of verbal

and nonverbal clues that may indicate his plans have not been frustrated.

10) Secure an agreement from the youth that he will talk to you if he begins feeling suicidal again.

11) Encourage him to take manageable, specific actions to change problem areas in his life.

12) Suggest professional counseling. Consult a local suicide prevention center (listed in either the White or Yellow Pages of the telephone book), a minister, school counselor, local mental health clinic, or hospital. However, let him know that this suggestion does not mean you are abandoning him.